DON'T STAY
in the
VALLEY

There's a Mountain to Climb

Anne Haughton

ISBN 979-8-89043-300-8 (paperback)
ISBN 979-8-89043-301-5 (digital)

Christian Faith Publishing
832 Park Avenue
Meadville, PA 16335
www.christianfaithpublishing.com

Printed in the United States of America

Thanks to my husband John Haughton for building it...
Thanks to Shane Jones for buying it.

Special thanks to the many ministries that kept me on the straight and narrow through the long, hard days. They seemed to know just what I needed and when. The dark days became a little brighter because of you.

Yael Eskstein
Jentzen Franklin
Matt Hagee
Rhonda Lazerte
Joyce Meyer
Jim Cantelon
Dr. David Jeremiah
Dr. Charles Stanley
Rev. Dr. John Tweetie
Joel Osteen
Doug Batchelor
Sid Roth
And many more

MY STORY IN A NUTSHELL

For twenty-six years, I worked alongside people with addictions. Drugs, alcohol, scratch tickets, and lottery tickets. I saw them as losers until one day God showed me that I, too, was addicted. Their addictions were open for all to see; mine was hidden and perhaps worse than theirs. Maybe, just maybe, I was the biggest loser of all.

CHAPTER 1

In pondering the idea of writing this book, one can only ask, "Where does one start to tell about the goodness of God?" The answer became very clear: Start at the beginning and go from there.

I was born at Port Clyde, Nova Scotia, in 1942. To say the least, times were tough. Dad worked on the railroad (CN) and Mom stayed home. Little did we kids know anything about a war that was raging in Europe. We were completely oblivious to bombs being dropped and thousands of people being killed every day. The Jews were being hunted down like dogs, loaded on trains, and shipped to concentration camps. To Hitler, the Jews were a little lower than humans and should be done away with. These precious people were being stripped of their very dignity. Not to mention homes, businesses, possessions, and their families.

While as a daily routine, thousands were being gassed or tortured, life went on as normal in my house. Dad went to work, Mom baked bread, date squares, cinnamon rolls and made homemade baked beans. Dad planted a large garden every year so there were enough pickles to last us over winter. Mom canned deer meat, and that was our Sunday suppers. The big woodstove in the kitchen sort of heated the whole house. That is, except where we slept. That is where the hot water bottles came in handy. We didn't have much but were happy and knew we were loved to a certain extent. Mom and Dad never hugged us kids (two older brothers), never kissed us, and not ever did I hear the words "I love you." Growing up, I didn't know there was such a word; I never heard it. We just sort of belonged to each other and together.

However, there was always food on the table and a bed to sleep in. Every September, we would get a new pair of sneakers for school. When I was about eight, there wasn't enough money for three pairs, so I was left out. I had to wear my brother's rubber boots. Being made fun of was not my cup of tea. Even at that age, I told myself that I would someday buy a dozen pairs of sneakers if I wanted to. I knew the way to success was hard work. That has stayed with me a lifetime.

Religion of any sort was not present in the home. No church, no Sunday school, no prayers. The one thing that I remember was we were not to swear. The mouth would be washed with soap if a curse word was used. Very early on, we learned that lying, stealing, cheating, and fighting would not be tolerated. The kindling was always sitting on top of the stove (up top), and all Mom had to do was point to it. Swearing was a definite no-no and was only used by adults if they thought things weren't going their way, at least the way they thought things should go.

As the years went on, Dad contracted TB and was sent to the sanatorium where he stayed for several years. TB was a common disease in the fifties and early sixties.

Dad was allowed to come home sometimes for the weekends. My little sister came along when I was ten. By then, there were four of us, ages baby, ten, eleven, and thirteen years of age. Somehow, we got by. Mom received the baby money of twenty-one dollars a month, and with my new sister arriving, that went up to twenty-eight a month. We all pitched in. In the summer, we kids picked blueberries and blackberries and went from house to house selling them. We received twenty-five cents a quart and usually made two or three dollars a day. After all, they really were fresh berries, sold the same day as picked. As a can of milk was ten cents and a pound of hamburger was twenty-five cents, we did okay. A few nights for supper, we crumbled up soda crackers, poured hot water over them to soften, then put sugar and milk over them. We didn't like it much, but our tummies were full. In the winter, we cut Christmas trees and sold them. For a small tree, we received twenty-five cents and a very large tree for fifty cents. A man came by in a truck and loaded them on. I will never forget dragging those trees out of the bush and how hard we worked.

On one occasion, we sold so many trees we made $17. We were so happy that our hard work paid off. Another lesson for me. Put your nose to the grindstone and work hard. That is the secret to success. We did just about anything to make a dime, even helping our neighbor split his firewood. That got us fifty cents. Dad took up leather craft in the hospital and made beautiful wallets, belts, and handbags. Mom would bring them home to sell. A leather wallet with your name engraved on it would bring $5. Wow!

Dad was out of the hospital now and back to work on the railroad, but not for long. Now in his late forties, he has lung cancer. My dad died at the age of fifty-two. The last thing he asked for was a cigarette. How sad! How strong the addiction!

Life went on at home. At the age of sixteen, I went to work at Roseway Hospital for the summer. I stayed in the dormitory with about twenty or more other women, some much older than myself. There were two sisters residing there who were different from the others. They read their Bibles and often talked about God. I was drawn to these two girls, but others were not necessarily interested in their Bible stories. They told me about the son of God whose name was Jesus. It seems as though back in the Old Testament times, people had to sacrifice lambs for remission of sins, but for thousands of years, this wasn't working. They just had to keep sacrificing animals. God needed a permanent solution for our sins. This kind of talk was all together new to me. What sin did I have in my life? I didn't kill anyone! I don't steal or lie. Those things were sin, I thought. As the days went on and we talked, they quoted a scripture to me after explaining to me those types as sins were not what they were talking about. They read Roman 3:23, "For all have sinned and fall short of the Glory of God." If all have sinned, then that must mean me too. "All people" means the entire world, and I'm one of them.

The sisters went back to the Old Testament at the time God created Adam (the first man) and Eve (the first woman). Genesis 2:4 tells us that the heavens and earth were made by God. He planted a garden in Eden, and there he put a man. God had planted trees of all sorts, pleasant to look at and good for food. In the middle of the garden, God put a special tree known as the tree of life and the tree of knowledge of good and evil. There, in the garden, Adam had free reign. He could enjoy and eat of the fruit (Genesis 2:16) but was told by God not to eat from the tree of knowledge of good and evil. If Adam disobeyed the warning and ate, he would surely die.

What was hard about that? After all, Adam had a whole garden of fruit to enjoy. So why not do what God says and live? In 2:18, we find, "It is not good for man to be alone. I will make him a helper suitable for him." But of all the living things God had made, such as beasts, birds, fish, and other living things, the most crafty was the serpent. In fact, the serpent was so crafty that he said to the woman, "Did God really say you must not eat fruit from that one particular tree?" But as we read in Genesis 1:19, the woman did eat from that tree disregarding what God, her creator, had commanded her not to do. Not only did she eat, she gave Adam, and he ate also. Right then and there, sin had entered into the world through one man's disobedience and has followed down the human chain of history.

I'm listening to the sisters as they read from their Bibles and tell the stories. I had never heard of such things. God was never spoken about in my home. We didn't go to church; in fact, I didn't know there was a God. I certainly didn't know that He created the very earth that I was walking on. Imagine I'm breathing the very air into my lungs that God made. He even created the lungs the air is going into. Wow!

After days of being asked to go to church with them, I finally gave in and went. Everyone seemed so happy to see me. It was as if they had known me forever. I loved the singing and looked around as everyone was smiling and clapping their hands to the music. I just had to learn more about this sin thing. If I really do have sin in my life, how do I get rid of it? If I have sin, these two sisters must have sin too.

Talking further over the summer, I found out that although they were not perfect people the sin of Adam (being born in sin) was gone. It was erased, gone for good, never to be remembered by God again.

> For I (God) will forgive and remember their sins no more. (Hebrews 8:12)

> For unto you (me) is born this day in the city of David, a Savior who is the messiah! (Luke 2:11)

> For God so loved the world that He gave His only begotten Son (Jesus) so that whosoever believes will not perish but have ever lasting life. (John 3:16)

That's very simple. Believe, accept, and go to heaven and not hell. The Bible tells us that salvation is so simple that people stumble over it.

> Jesus said you should not be surprised by me saying "You must be born again." (John 3:7–8)

> Jesus says "No one can enter the Kingdom of God unless they are born of the water and the spirit. Flesh gives birth to flesh but the Spirit gives birth to spirit." (John 3:15)

Finally, I believed Jesus was the Savior of mankind. All through the Old Testament, people lived by the law. Through Jesus's death on the cross, we enter the period of grace. Sin entered through Adam (the period of law). We now live knowing that Jesus removed that sin by giving His life (sacrificed freely for us, me). No more animal sacrifices; the price has been paid. No more bloodshed on the altars by lambs. Jesus took their place.

Hebrews 9:22 tells us that without the shedding of blood, there is no remission of forgiveness of sin. So when Jesus's blood was shed, my sins were forgiven if I believed. It all hinges on that word—*believe*.

A couple weeks later, I went to church with the sisters and gave my heart to Christ. I couldn't see God; I couldn't touch God. But I knew without a doubt that He was a Living Spirit and that He loved me. Along my life's path, I would remember a scripture I had learned: "Faith is the substance of things hoped for, the evidence of things not seen" (Hebrews 11:1).

Much later on in my senior years, this verse would come back to me over and over. There was something I hoped for and could not see a way this would happen. You will read of this in the following chapters.

After summer was over, I went home, and the two girls went to theirs.

CHAPTER 2

At the age of sixteen, I was eligible to get my driver's license. I was quite good at driving the farm tractor. Once in a while, Dad would let me drive his truck up and down the driveway. I had no trouble keeping it straight on the on path. I could even park it by backing up and not hitting the wagon. A friend of the family had an old half-ton truck and taught me how to use the gear shift. It was a long handle on the floor, and I had to press on the clutch to shift. I soon caught on, and away we went to the driver's exam. To this day, I can't remember where got the $7 from, but I paid the money and filled out a paper with my name, age, and address. The examiner got in, and away we went. I drove about a mile or so. As we were going up a steep hill, he told me to stop. I did so, and the truck was not supposed to roll backward when I started to go. I put the truck in D and released the clutch pedal with my left foot, all the time keeping my right foot on the gas pedal. I did good! No rolling backward. I was told to turn around in some guy's driveway and head back to the office. He signed a piece of paper and gave me my license. When I think of young people getting a driver's license nowadays, I shiver. If there was ever one thing in my life that I enjoyed doing, it was driving. It was like I had won a lottery whenever I could borrow Dad's truck to go to church. The driving of a vehicle would become one of the most important parts of my life. It would be a way of saving my life.

One of the sisters returned to normal college where she studied to be a teacher. The other sister went to Bible College in Rhode

Island and later become an RN. I will always be thankful for their patience and willingness to put up with all the questions, always forgiving me for the foolishness I presented to them.

CHAPTER 3

I drifted along, hating school, not caring whether I passed a grade or not. I had no reason to go to church now; the girls were gone. Some days, I remembered God and would say a prayer. On most days, I went on my merry way, dreaming of the time I could finally get out of Port Clyde and do something with my life. My dream was to own a grocery store. It never left my head. When I was young, maybe seven or eight years old, I would take all the cans and bottles out of the cupboard and sell them to myself for four or five cents. Canned milk cost ten cents. If I sold it for twelve cents; I would soon be rich. All my young life, I was a dreamer, but I eventually grew up and realized life is serious; it's not a game.

In 1960, at the age of eighteen, I wanted to join the army as my brothers had done. Mom just said, "If that's what you want, you will have to go to Halifax to join." Mom and I boarded the train in Port Clyde and headed to Halifax to the recruiting office. Once there, the interviewing officer asked me what I thought I would be best suited for. Did I want to be a nurse? A secretary? Or what! I told him, "I want to be a driver. Maybe they have openings to drive Jeeps. I could drive generals or whoever needed to get from place to place."

After a few short minutes he said that the army was not hiring at this time. "But," he said, "they are hiring at the air force office." I think that army guy just wanted to get rid of me. At the RCAF office, I was told I could join and was given tests to see what I was suited for. Tests showed that I was suited for radar operations. I signed up and was given my papers to return on a certain day. We went back home, and in two weeks, I boarded the train again bound for Halifax. There were dozens of girls waiting, and we were taken by bus to the train station. We were heading to St. Jean, Quebec, for basic training. We were on an adventure. This is what I've been waiting for. I'm finally leaving home, along with the other fresh faces just of school.

After basic training, a number of us went to Clinton, Ontario, for our trade training. I became a fighter cop (fighter control operator). After training, I was sent to St. Sylvestre for my posting. While there, I met another air woman who was a Christian. She had been there about six months before I arrived. She was also from the town where I went to church. She went to a different church. We became good friends and spent a lot of time together.

After our shifts were over, most of the girls would go to the corporals' club for drinks. They're eighteen or nineteen years old now, away from home, no mom or dad to supervise, so why not? Some would go to the gym and later to a movie on base. My friend and I loved broomball, volleyball, and basketball and could always get in a good game.

The barracks were usually empty in the evening so I started reading the Bible again, and we would thank God for His goodness. Sometimes we would go to the chapel. It felt like we were closer to God there. It was quiet there, and trust me, there was never anyone there except on Sundays. One night, as we were sitting on the platform's edge with our legs dangling down, I heard a sound at the back of the chapel on the left side. "Did you hear that?" I asked my friend.

She replied that she didn't hear a thing. "You mean you don't hear the rumbling of wheels on a cobblestone road?" I had to know.

"No, I don't hear a thing, but if you do, you must be having a vision."

As I sat there, I saw it all come into view. It was the most beautiful chariot pulled by a lone horse. The horse was well decorated as was the chariot. The horse and chariot came to a standstill, but the horse kept prancing. He wanted to go, but the driver held the reigns tight. Then as sure as I'm living, I heard a voice say to me "Come down." I was trembling but got up and walked to the chariot. There the voice said, "Come closer." I laid my hand on the side of the chariot, and as I did, I told Him, "I don't see anything."

He said, "Look deeper."

As I looked, it was not clear what I was looking at. Again He spoke, "Look deeper." I still couldn't tell what was in the chariot, and once again, for the third time, He spoke and said, "Look deeper."

I looked deep into the chariot and saw books. All kinds of books, all colored books. There were so many, and each book held a different story. As I looked, I said, "All I see are books, lots of books, all colored books." Some were used books as though many people had been reading them. Some were new. The chariot began to move, and I backed off and away. As I did, I saw and heard the chariot rumble along the cobblestone street until it disappeared.

I started walking back to the front of the chapel where my friend was sitting. I didn't know what just happened. But I knew what I saw and heard.

"Did you see that?" I asked my friend.

"No, I didn't see or hear anything. You were talking about books."

"Didn't you hear the wheels of the chariot?" I had to know.

"No, I didn't see or hear anything. Whatever it was you saw or heard was for you and you only, not for me." I related the whole thing to her, and lo and behold, she believed me. The meaning was not made clear to me until 2022, the time of the writing of this book. As you read, you, too, will catch what it was all about. That particular incident happened in 1962. Over sixty years ago. Over the years, I thought about it nearly every day or week. How many times did I wonder if it would ever know the meaning. In reality, I knew I would but just didn't see my life ahead of me to know when.

While still serving in the air force, my friend discussed going to Bible school in the US. I thought about it and decided I would apply also. We were both accepted, and after we left the service, we went to Long Island, New York, to Bible school. I studied there for two years and transferred to a school in Rhode Island. After graduation, I applied to a school in Florida. That particular school trained padres for the US armed forces. I thought I stood a pretty good chance as I served in the air force. I was accepted and received a BA degree in religious education. I never did become a chaplain. School was over.

Now what? Where do I go? What do I do? I could teach in a Bible school. No, that was not what wanted. I didn't want to study any longer or teach. I wanted to be free, go where I want, and do what I want. Should I go back to Nova Scotia? There's no work there, except the fish factories. No, that won't work.

I often heard that Ontario was the land of opportunity. You could get a job anywhere and make big money. After all, I'm sick of not having a dime in my pocket. I went to Toronto and worked in a nursing home there. In the meantime, I didn't have a health care aide certificate. It only took a few months of study, then I could work anywhere. I settled into my new life. I saved enough for a car and had my own place to live and food to eat. Church was not in my life full time. I would read the Bible once in a while. Very seldom go to church.

I was doing okay and didn't need any more religion. I needed God, and I knew He loved me, just not religion. If a problem came up, I knew where to find God. I would take Him off the shelf and expect His help. Although I was not intending to forget about God, sometimes I did. He never forgot about me. He is very present in the time of need.

CHAPTER 4

We are now up to the late 1960s. One afternoon at work, one of the nurses asked if I had ever gone to Woodbine racetrack to watch the horses. No, I never had. I never even heard of Woodbine. Would I like to go with her on my day off? Sure! I knew nothing about betting, but she showed me, and I caught on real quick. Place $2 to win, $2 to place (come in second), and $2 to show (come in third). If I do that, I'm sure to win something. Win, place, show. Two dollars was the minimum bet, but you could bet a hundred dollars if you liked. After the races were over, I discovered that I came out with $6 more than I went with. This seemed like a good thing. A sure way to make quick money, and I don't have to work for it. I couldn't wait to go again. I was chomping at the bit, but I want to go alone. I don't want anyone looking over my shoulder. I knew exactly what I was going to do. I had a bit of money in the bank, didn't go anywhere, didn't do anything, and it's nobody's business what I do with my money. I'm going to make $5 bets instead of $2. Over the months, they soon became $10 then $20 bets. A few times I tried $100 to win. Did I win? Not in a million years. I was losing, winning, losing. But there was always next time. My horse will come in, and I'll be rolling in the money. This betting thing seems to have control over me, and I didn't know how or didn't want to stop.

In the meantime, I heard of a nursing home in New Market, Ontario. It was more of a country setting. The town was about one and a half hours north of Toronto. It would be nice to get out of the big city, away from the hustle and bustle. Toronto was way too busy and big. Living in a city was certainly not like living in Port Clyde. I wanted to feel the rural area of Ontario.

On my day off, I drove to New Market and applied for the job. I got it! I gave my notice in Toronto, and after two weeks, I was working and enjoying my new apartment. I was twenty-eight years old and very much alone. I had started smoking by now. All the nurses smoked on their breaks. I guess I should too. Nearby my apartment was a convenience store where I picked up my smokes, pop, chips, and whatever else! There was always an older guy working. Sometimes we would talk a few minutes. I'd say stupid things like "Boy, cigarettes are expensive"—say, forty-seven cents. "Guess I should quit." He told me that would be a good idea. I told him, "Stop selling them then." Over time, we found out about each other. His wife passed away. He was left with two daughters to raise. One was married with kids; the other girl was with him. She was thirteen. What could I say about me? Boyfriend? No! Single? Yes! Do you date? Sometimes.

One night, as I was watching TV, I started thinking about this man; maybe he's right. Maybe I should quit smoking. As I continued to watch *Wild Kingdom* and having lit up my tenth cigarette or so, I started to think about my dad. Laying in a hospital bed dying of lung cancer and asking for a smoke. The half pack of smokes were staring me in the face. I got up, took the cigarettes out of the package, crumbled them, and down the toilet they went. That was my last cigarette.

Having quit smoking, I had no reason to go to that store anymore. When I finally did go, he asked why I hadn't come in for a while. He asked if I had been sick. I told him I hadn't been sick, and I didn't need to come because I had quit smoking. He seemed pleased. Over the next few weeks, I would go to his store a couple times a week. I had just turned twenty-eight.

"I don't suppose you would go to the Chinese restaurant with me," he asked. I had been going out with a guy from Toronto, but that relationship was going nowhere. I told him I would like to go. We found out each other's ages. His, forty-seven. Mine, twenty-eight. We began to see each other on a regular basis after that. Over the next few months, he spoke of marriage and wanted know if the age difference mattered to me. It didn't! I thought he was the nicest and kindest man I had ever met. He bought me gifts and always paid for diners, although I often offered. I believed the compliments he paid me was what sold me. He was Dutch Reformed, and I was…I don't know what. He talked freely about God and His goodness. I had never gone out with a true gentleman before, and it was quite a change. The guys I went out with were not even worth mentioning. By this time, he had proposed, and I said yes.

I would help him in his store on my days off. I would stock shelves and fill the milk cooler. I learned to do orders, and according to him, I was handy to have around.

One evening, I was breaking down boxes when his thirteen-year-old daughter came in the back room and started helping me. She had never mentioned that her dad and I were even getting married. I asked her, "Are you coming to the wedding?" It was two weeks away.

She threw the box down and asked, "What wedding?"

I was a little surprised! "Your dad's wedding, of course. We're getting married in two weeks."

Her dad was in the front of the store serving customers, but that didn't matter. She stomped out to the front of the store and yelled directly at her father. "Are you going to marry her?"

He smiled at the three or four customers and turned to his daughter, "I'll talk to you in a few minutes." I'm waiting for the last customer to leave, then it was going to be my turn. "Do you mean to tell me that you didn't tell her that we were getting married in two weeks?"

He waved me off with his hand. "She would have known in two weeks anyway." All I could do was stand there as he continued to move boxes and straighten up chocolate bars. I didn't know how I felt. I was disgusted and shocked. I turned and started walking out of the store. "Maybe you'd better go in the backroom. I hear your thirteen-year-old crying." I got in my car and drone to my apartment.

My thoughts were racing a mile a minute. I thought I knew this man. Why didn't he tell her? What was the reason behind it? Why was it a secret? Did he even tell his oldest daughter? Do I even want to marry this guy? Was I supposed to show up at his apartment in two weeks with all my belongings and just move in?

A few days passed, and finally he called to ask why I hadn't been around. I just told him I had things to think about. "Maybe you better come over tonight, and the three of us can sit down and get a few things straightened out."

Yeah, okay! The one thing I want to know first of all is, "Why did you ask me to marry you? Is there love involved in this thing?" Before this incident took place, I thought he was Mr. Wonderful. I was excited! I was looking forward to being a wife. Deep down in my innermost being, I had doubts. I couldn't bring myself to even tell my coworkers that I was even getting married. I kept it to myself. The only one who knew was a close friend I worked with, and she promised to keep quiet as she knew what was going on. She would be my bridesmaid, maybe.

I showed up for the meeting!

I went into the apartment, expecting to be told that she didn't want me in her father's life. They were sitting on the sofa, and I sat in a chair opposite. The first one to speak in a rather loud and demanding tone was the daughter.

"You're not going to be my mother!" So where is this coming from? Who mentioned that I even wanted to be? I sat there with my hands folded in my lap, looking down at them.

"I had a mother! She was the best mother in the world! She died, and you're not going to replace her!"

I'm waiting for her father to speak, so kept quiet. Finally! I did speak. "I'm sorry about your mom. I know you miss her. People tell me she was lovely. I could never take her place, nor would I want to. I'm marrying your dad and hope somehow we can be civil to each other and get along. Your guidance will be from your dad, not me. But…if I can help you in any way, I'll be here."

Here we go again! "You don't get it, do you? We're doing just fine without you in our lives!"

He reached out and touched her hands. "That's enough! We're getting married in two weeks, and that's all there is too it."

Just as I think I'm having a nightmare, she jumped up and goes out the door. She slams it so hard, the picture on the wall moved slightly. Meeting over, I guess.

What was I supposed to say now? "Well, that went rather well, don't you think?" He got up and stated that he had to go to the store—back to work. As he passed me, he just muttered, "She'll get over it!"

But the question is, will I? Things got a bit better between my intended and myself, and in 1971, we finally did get married, and yes, I did move in. All the staff were shocked when my big mouth friend started telling everyone. I could have told them myself, but I didn't get the chance.

Was the daughter speaking to me? Not on your life! You could cut the atmosphere with a knife. Should I cook for three people or two? Why do we sit at the dinner table, and she takes her plate to her bedroom? One night in particular stands out to me. We were having steak, so I asked her if she would be home for supper. Her answer was "For your record-keeping, no, I won't."

So I bought two steaks instead of three. Just as we were sitting down to eat, she came in. Her father asked if she was hungry, and she answered yes, she was a little. He grabbed another plate from the cupboard and put his steak on the plate for her along with extra vegetables. He pushed it toward her and said, "Here, you can have mine. I'm not really hungry." I saw red! I grabbed the plate from her, took it to the garbage disposal, and dumped it in. My plate followed! I grabbed my sweater and said ever so softly, "I feel a little hungry. Think I'll eat out tonight!" And that's what I did!

This marriage thing is not off to a good start. A few days later after being married for a week, he told me that he was going to Toronto for the day. Fine with me! He had to meet someone. Okay!

I was sitting on the sofa when he came in later that evening. He came over to me and handed me a dozen red roses. My heart skipped a beat. Finally, whoever he met in Toronto got him straightened out.

I took the roses, and as he started to take off his jacket, he said, "You may as well have these. I was dating a woman in Toronto and wanted to tell her I was married now. She wasn't home, so you enjoy them." Have you ever had a stunned moment? I think that is what I had. He went to Toronto to see a woman; she wasn't home so I may as well have the roses. I sat there for a few minutes and the only thought I had was "This marriage is really, really not going to last too long." He came back into the living room, and I got up and went outside still holding the roses. I opened his car door, ripped the roses to shreds, and threw them all over his car. They flew on his seat, the dashboard, the floor, the backseat, and the back window. When I returned to the apartment, he asked me where the roses were. "Oh, they're in a safe place."

He was very upset with me the next day. He always made a bank deposit in the mornings. I guess he must have done so as he was very upset when he returned. I was sitting, waiting for him. He came in and glared at me. "I had no idea I married a child." I turned the TV on.

This was my marriage for several years. His daughter was now married, and we had moved to Toronto. He had taken a meat-cutting course and after a while applied to become a meat inspector with the federal government. I continued to work in the nursing home, now back in Toronto. I also started my horse-racing thing again. I didn't know how much I missed the gambling. I never bothered to mention it as he wouldn't care anyway. I thought I could get through anything now that I had my outlet. Somehow it would excite me and make me happy for a few hours.

Things were not too bad until I came home one evening after the shift was over at 11:00 p.m. I couldn't begin to explain the way I felt when I opened the door, and the apartment was empty. The few things left were my bed, a night table, my clothes, and a coffee table with a note. "Don't try to find me and don't bother my kids. They won't tell you anything!"

I did phone his oldest daughter, and she told me nothing. She was sorry!

Now I have to downsize and find a small apartment. Money wasn't a problem as I was a good saver. I sat on the bed and asked God, "Why?" That's all I could say. I knew the answer. Did I ask God about this man? Did I ask God if he was the right one? Did I even know God anymore or even know that He loved me? God wanted to be a part of my life, but I had forgotten Him. God had been put on the shelf again. Now I was to take Him down, dust Him off, and be friends. What a pitiful life I've been living. Have I even been living or just existing?

I found a small apartment and continued to work. I put on a good face and kept quiet. Work and the race track. That was my life now. I had a phone installed, and wouldn't you know it? Who called? Yes, you're right! How was I doing? Am I okay? Can we meet for a coffee? Meet for a coffee! Why? What is it that he has to talk about that is important to me?

I met him at Country Style Donuts. Always the gentleman, he opened the door and bowed as I went in. I won't lower myself to ask why he wanted to meet. I'll wait for him to tell me. Finally, after talking about nothing, he said he needed a change in his life. "I thought there would be a big fight if I told you I was leaving, so I just left." He was wrong! I really had had enough and would have told him so. However, he didn't give me the chance. "Can I take you to dinner some time?" Now, here's the thing. Am I completely stupid?

Over the months, it became a regular thing. After eight months, he asked if we could try again. What do you think I said? Yup, you're right. I said yes.

We gave up both our apartments and got a nice three-bedroom in Weston, north of the city.

In the evenings, he would sit and read the *Toronto Star* newspaper for hours. He sometimes circled things. I thought nothing of this, just that it was odd.

It's getting on to 1980 now. He works! I work! I also have a part-time job to feed my habit. I was very busy. We had been back together for a few years now, and he was still at the newspaper thing. Only now he was staying late at work two or three nights a week.

My girlfriend was visiting for a few days and wondered why he was circling things in the newspaper. I just shrugged my shoulders. I had no idea. He always took the newspaper with him and would go for a walk every evening. My friend asked, "Where does he go, and why does he take the newspaper?" She suggested that one evening we should follow him at a distance. We did! He walked to the main post office, opened a box with his key, and took out letters. He put them in the inside pocket of his jacket. We quickly hid and followed him home. Why does he have a PO box? We have our own at the apartment by the elevator. We waited until he went to bed. She watched as I checked his jacket pocket for a letter. I read it! "I can get away for a few hours on Wednesday evening. Can we meet at the usual?"

I can't believe this! What in the world is going on? Wait, just wait. Let's see if he will be working overtime on Wednesday.

Yup! He came home very late and was very tired! The job is so demanding.

I let it go! For now! Tomorrow, we'll have a talk. Not that I'll hear the truth. No, that will never happen.

I waited until he spread the newspaper on the table and picked up the pen.

"What's that one's name, the woman you just circled?"

"What are you talking about? I'm looking for part-time work."

"Where were you Wednesday after work?"

"I was at work, overtime!"

"No, you weren't. When I phoned the plant, they said you left at 5:00 p.m."

"What is this? What are you getting at? I stopped for dinner with some friends, and we talked a long time."

"You know, don't you, that I don't want to stop you from being happy? So if other women make you happy, then why am I here?"

He got up and went out. He didn't come back that night. The next day, I went to work. Somehow, I got through the day. I didn't care whether I went home or went to the moon. I was at the end of the line and didn't know where to turn or what to do.

I shouldn't have worried about it because when I got home, the apartment was empty—again! Will I never learn? I had my bed, clothes, and small kitchen table. This time—no note. I think I felt relief. For some reason, I could smell freedom. Back to a small apartment with my bed, clothes, and kitchen table. I didn't miss him and didn't care where he was or who he was with. I was happy to be alone, away from the lies and deceit.

In 1982, while helping a friend in her convenience store, a well-dressed man came in with papers in his hand. He shoved them at me, asked me my name, and told me to sign the papers. Well, no, I was not about to sign anything. He left them on the counter and left.

I opened them and read "Divorce." I smiled for the rest of my shift. I said, "For better or for worse" but I didn't have any "better," and the "worse" was over. I was free and would never see his face again. No more lies, ever.

CHAPTER 5

My life was once again peaceful. I had a bit of money in the bank and could go to the races whenever I wanted; my world was okay.

Through the years, I would remember God. I would think back to when I gave my heart to Jesus all those years ago. How did God put up with my foolishness? Why does He love me even when I forget Him or think I don't need His guidance? I now worked the overnight shift at the nursing home, 11:00 p.m.–7:00 a.m. I would come home, catch a few hours' sleep, get up, and hit the racetrack. It was always the next time. Tomorrow I'll win; I'll come in big. Why? I didn't need the money. I was healthy, strong, and willing to work double shifts if they needed me. The racetrack became my second home. Winning a few bucks, losing more, it didn't matter; it was my outlet. It kept me sane. I just didn't care!

Somehow, I had time for a few dates. I don't know what they called themselves, but I had a name for most of them—losers. I had gone out with one guy three or four times. Nothing serious, at least on my part. He had other ideas. A knock came on my door one evening, and when I opened it, he stood there. Two large suitcases stood nearby. "What are you doing? What's going on? Why the suitcases?" I asked.

"Can I come in?" I moved back, so he could enter. "I've decided to move in with you, and we can split the cost of everything. It will be a win-win situation."

"I hate to upset the apple cart, but I don't think so. In fact, I know so."

He just could not see what the problem was. After he drank his coffee, he wanted to know what he was supposed to do now. He gave up his room and had no place to go. Was this somehow my problem as I had not been consulted in the first place. Reluctantly, he left. I never saw him again.

I would sometimes go for a coffee and sit and think. There was one guy whom I talked to quite often. He always seemed to be there. After a few weeks of talking, he asked me a question. But first, he explained that he was married and had six kids. "I take it you're not married," he began. "I see you here all the time, alone. I wonder if you would like to be my 'Wednesday night'?"

I wasn't sure what I just heard. Does that mean he has six nights covered, but Wednesday is open? Over the years, I guess I just became accustomed to crap. "What would your wife say?"

"Oh, she wouldn't have to know."

"Well then, I'm afraid I'll have to decline your offer."

He shrugged his shoulders. "Okay, your loss."

That's how my life was moving. Horse races, work, and a few dates. There were a few more interesting episodes, but I'll just remember them—not so fondly.

CHAPTER 6

In the summer 1986, I was still working full-time but helping my friend in her store part-time. I worked a few hours in the evenings to give her a break. I would leave around 10:00 p.m. to go the nursing home, a thirty-minute drive through traffic.

I was reading my Bible again and prayed often. I wondered if God heard me, but I know He did. I started back to church by now and was attending Evangel Temple in Toronto. It was a large church and was always packed. For some reason, I thought I was a Christian again. But in reality, I was far from it. I had one foot pointing toward God and His goodness and the other foot pointing toward my own selfish wants and wishes.

One evening, while working at my friend's store, a guy came in. I hadn't seen him before. I figured he weighed around four hundred pounds. He was unshaven, had dirty hair, and smelled of beer. His work clothes looked like they hadn't been washed in a year. He asked for two packs of smokes. I sold them to him, and he left. I mentioned him to my friend. She said, "Oh, that must've been drunken John."

The very next day, he came back, same clothes, same condition. He asked for his regular smokes. Only this time, he mentioned that he was a bit short on cash and asked if he could charge them till payday. I asked him where he worked. Looking and smelling like he did, I couldn't imagine where he worked or who would ever hire him. He shrugged his shoulders and said, "Oh I'm a carpenter. I work here and there." No! I didn't let him charge the smokes.

He said, "Okay, I understand," and left.

He came in quite often, and we began talking, small talk. I found out his wife was near death (cancer), and he would visit her after he finished work. He sure didn't shave or comb his hair before he went. Maybe he's grieving, knowing she soon will be gone. Maybe life hasn't been kind to him. I told him a bit about my life and that I attend church every Sunday night. I was a little reluctant to tell him he would be welcome to come with me. I jokingly told him he might have to shave and change his clothes. We left it at that.

A few nights later, there was a commotion outside the store. It seems as though John was really drunk, and a couple of guys were trying to take his keys from him. The guys won. They brought the keys in and asked me to see that he gets them tomorrow. John staggered away down the street.

A few times when he came in, I noticed that his clothes were clean. He was losing weight. He mentioned that his wife had passed away. I was so sorry for him. I somehow felt the loss.

After that, I didn't see him all summer. I asked around but no one had seen him. No one knew where he had gone or what had happened to him.

I thought that was too bad. He probably is a nice guy under the filth and rags. He was polite and easy to talk to. What could have gone so wrong in a person's life that made them to just give up? Just not care if you shower, if you're clean, if you don't stink. Don't they care what others think? Maybe he had to be drunk every day—to forget! But life goes on. What was it that he couldn't accept or cope with? Guess I'll never know.

CHAPTER 7

After months of not seeing John, he suddenly appeared. It was my day off from the nursing home (Sunday), and I was working day shift for my friend. That would give her time with her family, and I would make it to church in plenty of time.

The store was quiet. I was filling shelves when the door opened, and a nice-looking guy walked in. He was wearing a dark-blue suit, a white shirt and tie, and brand-new black shoes. His face was clean-shaven, and he had short hair nicely combed. He was a big guy, around 250 pounds, I guessed, and about six feet.

I left the shelf and went to the front, all the time staring at this guy. I guess I made him feel uneasy. The first words either of us spoke was by him.

"Are you going to church tonight?"

"John, is that you?" I was still looking him over.

"Yes, I am!" I said.

"Would it be okay if I came with you?" It was beyond belief. "Where have you been? What happened to you?"

"I've been away for a while doing some soul searching."

He turned to leave but stopped before opening the door. "I've stopped drinking and smoking. I was beginning to really like you, but I didn't think a lady like you would want anything to do with me." He opened the door. "I'll come back at six."

When I saw him at six o'clock, I asked where his van was. "Oh, they [the police] towed it as it wasn't road-worthy." I had seen his van so I believed him. It was what I call a raddle trap. I wondered how it stayed together. The van was mostly blue with a green fender and red passenger door.

Besides the fact that the windshield had a long crack in it, the van wasn't too bad. The next question was, "Do you miss your van?" He smiled and shook his head in a no motion. I owned a new Chevy Impala and asked if he would like to drive, and he didn't hesitate. The next time I went to work for my friend, she wanted to know who the guy was that was in the car with me. I told her it was John. Her mouth flew open in disbelief. "You mean drunken John, cigarette John?"

"Yes, it was that John." She kept staring at me with her mouth open.

While driving to church, John explained he had been away getting help with his life, as he called it.

"So you quit drinking, did you?"

"'Three moths sober and don't want to drink—ever again."

"And smoking too?"

"Yup!"

I have heard this story a dozen times. How long will this last? You just don't quit drinking and smoking overnight. And especially cigarettes. Wait a minute. I quit overnight. It is possible. But it was so. For the rest of his life, he never touched alcohol or smoked again.

"Don't you have a desire to pick up a beer or cigarette?"

"I have no desire whatsoever. I don't even think about it."

To my way of thinking, that was a miracle.

John and I often went out to dinner and continued going to church. I had a hard time getting past the ragged John. The one I so often saw stagger into the store. Instead he wore slacks and T-shirts, and his cologne smelled so good.

He spoke to me about accepting the Lord into his life. I left it up to him. When you feel you're ready, then that will be the time. One Sunday night, he accepted the Lord as his Savior. He said that he had lived in hell all his life and had no desire to go there after he died. He was serious and even bought himself a new black Bible. He couldn't understand it as he started reading in Revelation. I got him on track and mentioned he should start reading the book of John.

All I saw from John I liked. He was really different from that other guy I had married. He was a general contractor and could build a house from the ground up. He did plumbing, electrical, dry wall, roofing—you name it, he knew how to do it.

Little did I know, at the time, all his knowledge would come into play in the coming years. He was never around during the day, so I supposed he was on a job somewhere. He always had money to spend these days.

Months later, while dining at a steakhouse, he took a small box out of his pocket, opened it, and asked me to marry him. I just sat there and stared at him and the ring. "It's okay," he said. "Will you think about it? I know for sure that I love you. I want to be with you forever, but if you're not sure, it's okay."

I really liked John, and sometimes I felt that I loved him too. I was so afraid. I don't want to get in another mess. After all, I'm forty-four now, and he's forty-seven. I really didn't know what to do. I just couldn't go through another marriage like the first. He sat the ring on the table. It sat there all through dinner. Finally, I told myself to take a chance. I held out my hand and said, "Yes! I'll marry you." I still hadn't told him that I loved him. That didn't seem to matter. I don't think I knew what love was. I found it hard to say those words. To me, love was special. It was deep rooted and was supposed to last a lifetime. But did I know? I guess I must have told him at some point as we were married on December 19, 1986. In total, there were seven people at the wedding. What a perfect number.

Again, I did not pray for God's will in this matter. If I did, I don't remember. I was used to doing things on my own my way. I didn't need to ask permission or guidance in my life. How arrogant! John moved into my apartment. I was actually happy. I hadn't felt that in a long time.

Shortly after Christmas, a few days after we married, a man knocked on the door looking for John. I thought it was about a job. I told him John was at work and would he back around 6:00 p.m. He left, stating that he would return at six. As he walked away, he turned and said, "You think John is at work? Give your head a shake." What in the world does that mean? John came in at suppertime. He put his lunch bucket on the counter and washed up.

"Did you go to work today?"

Just then, the guy was back knocking on the door. I had knots in my stomach. John answered the door and said to the guy, "Go outside. I'll talk to you there." The man brushed by John and came into the apartment.

"No, not outside John, I'm going to talk to you in front of your wife."

John stood there, not saying a word. I was all ears. The guy was angry. "I want the eleven hundred you owe me, and I want it now."

"I don't have it right now, but I'm back to work, and I'll get it to you!" The man was red in the face.

"How, will you get it? I went to the job site where you work. They said you were fired two weeks ago. Furthermore, John, what about the seven hundred you owe Ted and the three hundred you owe Bruce? God only knows how much more you owe and to who. I'll be back on Friday for the money—all the money, not just a dollar."

He then looked at me. "Lady, you seem very nice, but why you married this loser is beyond me." He opened door to leave. "Friday, John, eleven hundred."

I left my dinner on the table and went to the living room. A few minutes later, John came in and sat by me. He didn't say a word, so I waited. When I couldn't stand it any longer, I asked him, "Do you have anything to say?"

"I don't know what to say."

"Well, it just so happens that I do know what to say. I've been through this crap before. You know what I'm talking about. When you leave here every morning with your lunch bucket, where do you go?"

"I just go out and look for work. The construction bosses all know me and won't hire me because of the drinking."

"You've been living a lie from the very first day we went to church months ago. Where did the money come from for the new suit, the new shoes, and most importantly, for this ring I've been wearing so proudly?"

"I borrowed the money from my old drinking buddies or wherever I could get it."

As you are reading this book, what would you have done? There were lies on top of lies, deceit on top of deceit. Was it possible that I was completely blind? That I didn't suspect anything was amiss? He had won me over by his kindness and willingness to change. I never ever suspected such dishonesty.

"How much do you owe these people?" He shrugged his shoulders and finally had an honest answer.

"I don't know! Thousands, I guess."

I sat and thought for a minute. "How did you expect to pay these people back? Didn't you think you had to? What kind of person are you, John? Do you think it's okay to treat me like this? What about God? You supposedly gave your heart to Jesus, your life to God? Was that a bunch of bologna too? Was it for show? Did you want to impress me? As far as I know, God doesn't like to be used by such foolishness."

John shook his head back and forth. "No! When I said I loved you. It's because I do love you. I have learned to love God, and I believe He helped me to stop my bad habits. I want a life with you. You're honest, kind, everything you do just right, and if you want the truth, I have a problem."

He sure got that right. John went on. "All my life, I've lied. Lied to friends, my family, and just about everyone I've come in contact with. I found, over the years, I could get just about anything by lying. I'd give my friends sob stories. They knew I was an alcoholic, and they would give me $100 or $200. Why should I work? It was easy money. I did work from time to time, but when I didn't show up because I was drunk, I got fired. I paid the rent and other bills. The rest went to the bottle. I am truly sorry! Do you think I'm worth helping?"

That was food for thought. Was he worth helping? And how does one go about that? Did I even want to bother? No! Not really. Do I have what it would take to help this man? John started to cry. He just held his head in his hands as the tears rolled down.

"John, do you want me to pay that eleven hundred dollars for you on Friday?" He straightened up fast and said, "No! I'll go talk to him tomorrow! I'll explain to him that I haven't had a drink in months. You would think he could see the difference in me. I'll see if he can find me a job, go out on a limb for me."

"Okay, but what about us? Can I trust you from now on? Have you ever told me the truth about anything?"

He came and sat closer to me. "Yes, there was one thing that was truthful. I said 'I love you,' and I know in my heart that is the truth."

John did go to see the guy the next day. After they talked, the guy said he knew of a position as an apartment maintenance man. He got the job! He also was able to pay the money back. I'm not sure the other people were ever paid back as there were too many.

He was like a kid when he brought home his first paycheck. He signed it and gave it me. That, at least, was a start on his part. He felt good about himself for the first time in years. We used a bit of his money to go out to dinner. Whenever he started to tell me about certain things, I would stop him, "If it isn't the truth, don't say it." More often than not, we would sit quietly. He went for counselling at the church for a few weeks, and soon we began to find things to talk about.

We talked often about leaving the city and going north to a small town. No one would know about his past, and carpenters were always in demand. With his knowledge, he would find work quickly.

I would quit my job here and find work in the town somewhere. After a few months, we heard of a bakery and doughnut shop for sale in Muskoka. We bought it with the money I had saved and soon bought a small three-bedroom house. It was old, but we were happy to have it.

When the lease was up at the bakery, we didn't resign. We closed the doors, and John started into what he really loved—carpentry. I was hired on at the nursing home.

John was bringing money home, and I supposed everything was fine. Until! The phone calls started. When is John coming to finish my bathroom? Where is John? Is he going to finish my basement? Is he going to finish my deck?

What in the world was going on? I confronted John, and he explained that carpenters always took on lots of jobs and did a bit of work on each one until the jobs were finished. That way, he always had work. He took money upfront to secure the job, and when it got finished, it got finished, simple as that. He didn't know whether he was coming or going.

After we came home from church one Sunday, I asked him, "What do you think God thinks of the way you do business?"

"I guess He is not too pleased with me. I'll finish off the jobs I have started then just take one job at a time." He did finish the jobs, but people were so angry they only paid half if at all. Serves him right!

CHAPTER 8

In 1990, after living in our house for four years we talked about building a few rooms on the back of the house. We could rent them out and have extra income. John could build it himself so it would just cost us for materials. I could certainly carry two-by-fours or pass him a hammer. There was only one problem with our idea. And it was a big problem. We lived in a residential neighborhood, and the neighbors might not be too happy with a rooming house on their street. The street was not zoned commercial. We would need permits to build. The town would need to know about our plans. I didn't think there would be a chance in a million for the town to give us a permit. We sort of forgot about it for a while. One evening while watching TV, John turned to me. "You know, Anne, if we could do this, it would be extra income for you if anything happened to me."

The next morning, John went to the town hall to the planning department. He told the guy what we wanted to do. He was told that he would have to attend a town-hall meeting to discuss our plans. He went on a Tuesday night before the council. John spoke and explained what we want to do. They said they would discuss it further and let him know. On Friday, he got a call from the planning department, asking if John could come down this morning. When he got there, the guy gave John the permit. He explained that our property and only our property was zoned as a duplex. We could build eight units (rooms). We couldn't believe it. There was no shortage of people needing a place to live.

Another problem. Where do we get the money to build? We needed a bulldozer to level the ground and dig the hole for the basement. Truckloads of cement. There was no thought of praying about it, but looking back now, the hand of God was in it all.

If you think our neighbors on our street were happy, think again! If you think they asked if we need help, think again! They were very busy, though, making phone calls to the town hall. Everyone was up in arms and ready for war.

As for John and me, we saw extra income, and if anything did happen to John, then I wouldn't have any worries. We went right on with our plans. The neighbor on our left demanded, "Don't you dare cut down those two maple trees." The neighbor to our right said, "Don't you dare take one inch off my property." It was going to be a battle, and a battle it was. The neighbors walked slowly by to see what was happening. Window shades were pulled back. The work permit was posted in our living room window, and many times we would see them reading it. The town gave us permission, and that's all there was to it.

We started in 1991 with the arrival of a bulldozer. As we worked at our regular jobs to make money, we would buy a load of two-by-fours or two-by-sixes or maybe a load of plywood. We paid for materials as our money came in. Each week, saw a truck unloading something. Windows, doors, trim, drywall—we needed it all.

John and I finished our regular jobs. We would eat supper then build until 9:00 p.m. or so. I carried the two-by-fours and measured out sixteen-inch centers, and he did the nailing. The floors were in, the walls went up, and the roof went on. Months of slugging and hammering. If it rained now, it wouldn't matter; we would stay dry. It was beginning to look like a building. The rooming house part was attached to the main house. All we had to do was open our back door and could step into the rooming house. Very convenient! John did the wiring, plumbing, and put in the windows and doors. There were four rooms downstairs and four upstairs.

A few neighbors softened a bit and wanted to have a look and see as to how things were going. We always let them have a look around.

Finally, the inspections were completed (electrical and plumbing). Now we could paint, put on door handles, and finish it completely. The place looked like a million dollars. It took the two of us four years to complete, and every nail and screw was paid for. We didn't owe a cent to anyone. There were eight rental units on two floors with a bathroom on each and a kitchen.

The rooms were furnished with a single bed, dresser, comfy chair, chair and table, and lots of shelves. All they had to do was bring their own TV. Cable wire had been installed in each room and was free for the tenants.

We received our occupancy permit in late 1994, and it took less than a week to fill the rooms. The rent was $325 a month, which gave us $2,600 a month of extra income.

There were eight different rooms. It was chaotic! Some had mental issues; there were alcoholics, drug users, and you name, we had it.

A few times, I complained to John about the smell of marijuana coming into our living room, but I didn't get too far.

"I built this place for you so you could have a nice income. It's yours. You collect the rents, you have the money, so you take the headaches." And that was that.

CHAPTER 9

By this time, I had quit working. A new Las Vegas–style casino had opened just one hour south from us. John and I took (my idea) many trips to Atlantic City or Las Vegas to gamble. He wasn't much of a gambler but went along with me. He would play until he won his money back and then stop playing. He would go to restaurants or sight-see.

Not so with me! I just had to keep playing. Five hundred, a thousand, it didn't matter. I cannot remember one time that I went home with money. But that's okay. There was always next time. It would be so depressing but was so exciting. One of these days, a machine will hit!

In 1995, John pulled up in front of our door and was driving a car with a taxi sign on top of it. He got out and came inside.

"Why are you driving a taxi?"

"Oh, I bought the car from a guy. I'm starting my own taxi business."

In the first place, there was already a taxi company in town. And don't you need a taxi license? What about insurance? He had been to the town hall and had five licenses. So far, only one car. Everything was on the up and up. What about an office and a dispatcher, wouldn't you need those? Would the other taxi company be happy? I don't think so. As far as the dispatcher, well he was just going to use his phone for now!

Was I a little shocked? You might say so. I guess I just stood with my mouth wide open.

"Did it even occur to you to discuss this with me? You do know that a taxi company means twenty-four hours a day, don't you? It's like seven days a week."

Did I marry this guy? Who is he anyhow?

"You have the rooming house for income. I just thought I'd make a bit extra also."

"Won't you need an extra driver so you can have a break?"

I knew it was coming. I knew exactly what he was going to say next.

"I figured you can drive if you want to. You can keep the money. You told me a dozen times you love to drive."

John drove and stayed awake two days and nights. He was so busy. People knew John (not the Toronto John), and they respected him. Finally, John hired another driver, and they would take shifts. How were they getting calls? I knew the taxi number was on the car and people could see it. I asked him who was taking the calls. Who is your dispatcher? Do you have an office? I soon realized why he hadn't told me.

Although she was married, that didn't stop her from having her flings. She was dispatching from her and her husband's apartment. John was warned to watch her by a couple of drivers from the other cab company. Her reputation was well known. When she was finished with a guy, she found a way to hurt them. Her husband didn't seem to mind. I had another question for John.

"Where did you meet her, and why would you hire her?"

"She's okay."

Yes, I really did marry this guy. He went to church twice on Sunday and, if possible, went on Wednesday nights.

Does he not know anything? The taxi customers thought it was strange that John had hired her and told him so.

Although, I must say, she had the voice of an angel.

It didn't take long for the company to grow. Soon, there were two cars and then five. Prices were cheap, and the calls kept coming. By this time, I was driving and was enjoying it. I was making good money. My shifts were always days, so that gave me the evenings for our new casino. There were around 2,500 machines, and it was huge!

Sometimes John would go and take five or six others, and they gave him $5 each. That way, he didn't have to pay for the gas out of his own pocket.

After some time, we heard of a lady who used to dispatch for the other company but had quit. She was happy to dispatch for us. John took the radio system out of the woman's apartment and rented a regular office. The lady we hired stayed with us until we sold the company eleven years later.

We had day, evening, and night dispatchers. I would dispatch on my days off. The first dispatcher with the not-so-hot reputation threatened John that if he fired her, he would be sorry. The money was rolling in, and I kept all the money I made. Usually one to three hundred a day. The other drivers gave John 40 percent of what they made.

Some weeks, John made over three thousand dollars. He always paid his tithe of 10 percent to the church. It was fine with me, but I had no idea how much he was really giving.

We are now up to eleven taxis. Sometimes, there wasn't enough money for repairs. The mechanic would let him charge the work, and John would pay later. When the bill got up the $10,000, I thought it was time to have a talk to John.

Where was the money going? Why was he always broke? The answer was simple! He was giving thousands to the church, and lo and behold, some of his money was going to his first dispatcher. He had been paying her every week so she wouldn't accuse him of, well, bad things. We got a few things straightened out. Only 10 percent now to the church. No more to our not-so-ladylike former dispatcher, and he paid the mechanic.

I asked John, "How did it go when you said you would not be paying her any more money?"

"Not so well! She just said, 'You stop paying me, you'll be a very sorry man.'" We left it at that as I thought it was just talk.

CHAPTER 10

I can't believe it's been ten years since John bought the taxi company. Time flies!

It's 2005. Most of my money is going to the casino. The rooming house was always full. One moves out; one moves in. It's a merry-go-round. Most of the tenants were alcoholics or drug addicts. Some went to work and lost their jobs. Some wives threw their husbands out. Some were ex-convicts. It was a mixed-up mess. Rents by this time was $475 a month, $3,800 a month. With that income and driving taxi, I found myself taking thousands of dollars to the casinos. By this time, there were two casinos.

The taxi business was booming. I sort of got John straightened out with the money problems. He now had money. I took over paying his bills for him, and he was doing well. He loved to eat out and would talk to all his friends. It would have been interesting to hear some of the conversations, I'm sure.

This former dispatcher was becoming a problem. She called the office, and each time, she requested that John pick her up and drop her off at the tavern. I didn't know about this for some time. Our dispatcher asked me one day, "What is this thing with so-and-so? Every time she phones for a ride, she requests John."

"Does she phone often?" I asked.

"Four or five times a week, sometimes twice a day."

Will this never stop? Again, I confronted John. Over the years, he kind of learned to tell the truth. Half and half, anyway.

"When she calls for a ride, who usually picks her up?"

"She asks for me, so I'm sent to drive her!"

"Where do you usually take her three or four times a week?"

"To the tavern. She calls for me 'cause she doesn't have any money."

"So you drive her to the tavern. She goes in for her beer, but she doesn't have any money. How does that work?"

John was getting angry and began to raise his voice. "Yes, I give her free rides and money for her beer. Is that what you wanted to hear?"

"What I want is for this to stop." John turned toward the door to leave.

He just said, "Whatever!" John had never talked to me this way before. I was surprised and disgusted. I sat for a while, thinking. Should I pray? I don't think God is too interested in me anymore. I'm as hopeless as John is. What a pain. For better, for worse, for sicker, for poorer. I just don't know anymore. When John came home that evening, I told him I wanted to talk.

"Yeah, I guess!" was his reply. We were sitting facing each other.

"You say you love me, then here's what I want you to do. Never drive her again or give her another red cent. If you continue to drive her, you can move out. It's up to you."

He didn't even look at me, just stared at the floor.

"And that's the way it's going to be, is it?" he finally spoke.

"Yes, John, that's the way is has to be. Your reputation is on the line." He stood up and went to the bedroom and came back with a suitcase and walked out the door.

Somehow, I felt relief. I'm so tired of babysitting. John had just turned sixty-seven years old. He had been through two hip replacements; he was a diabetic and was beginning to have other health problems. I bowed my head and prayed to God. I need help; he needs help.

I drove to the casino and parked in valet. I was spending so much money by now I didn't have to park way out in the parking lot. I had free buffets, and every week, I could stay at the casino hotel free of charge for two nights. I could forget everything! I only had one thing on my mind. Win that big jackpot.

I don't think anyone even knew that John had moved out. The dispatcher could reach him on his cell phone if she needed him. I hadn't talked to John for a few days. I heard over the car radios as he was given calls, and I suppose he heard me. One afternoon, I pulled my car up next to his as he sat drinking his tenth or twelfth coffee of the day. I asked how things were going and where he was living.

"I'm living with her and her husband." What! Did I hear right? He's living with her. I drove off without saying a word. Did I care? Well, sort of, I guess.

Five days later, he came to our house. He wanted to come home.

"That woman is disgusting. She walks around the house with nothing on. She is completely nude." I pictured this in my mind. She is over sixty, weighs 250 pounds, and sort of bounces when she walks. No wonder he wants to get away from that.

"Is that the only reason you want to come home?"

"I need help! I don't know what's wrong with me. I can't stand myself. It seems like there is almost no reason to live. I do such stupid things and have no answer for why. I love you so much, but you'd never know it, would you?"

I felt pity for John. Pity or disgust, I didn't know which was stronger.

What could I say?

"Come home if you want. I'll move upstairs, and you can live down here. I don't want to be hurt anymore by you. You go your way, and I'll go mine."

He showed up in an hour with his stuff. After work, I came home and went upstairs, and he sat in his recliner and slept.

It went that way for a while. One evening, I heard talking downstairs and went down. A police officer was talking to John. We both knew this officer as he attended the same church as John.

I asked what was going on. Nothing should shock me, but it did. The officer said a complaint of sexual harassment (rape) was laid against John by a certain party and that he (the officer) was put in charge of the case. John had to go to the police station for a mug shot and fingerprints. He had to go within two days.

John called the officer by name and said, "You know I would never do anything like that."

Then I asked, "Don't you know John? He wouldn't harm a flea."

"Yes, I know," the officer replied. "But my hands are tied. She keeps phoning the detachment, demanding that John be charged. She phones five or six times a day. The only way I can get her off my back is to charge John."

To my way of thinking, this was not a very good reason to charge someone with such a serious crime. I have asked myself a hundred times if things could get worse; well, they just did! The officer spoke to John. "I'm sorry about this. I know you are not guilty. Everyone in the church knows you. You are just a great guy. See you on Thursday." He left. John and I stood in the kitchen.

"Don't you even ask? You know me! You also know that I never touched that woman." I did know! I knew beyond a shadow of a doubt that he never touched her or would even think to do such a thing. It came back to me now. When John didn't need her to dispatch any longer, she told him, "If you fire me, you'll be sorry. You'll pay." There wasn't much sense to give her money any longer. She did the same thing to a driver from the other company. He had a trailer in Florida and with him found guilty he couldn't enter the US anymore. Now we have to sit back and wait. I felt sorry for John. I wondered how many other men paid the price because a woman was vindictive. It seems that men are automatically guilty whether they are or not. So sad! The local paper put the news on the front page: "Taxicab owner charged with 3 counts of sexual assault." Of course, his name had to be there. When the town hall heard of this, they called John. No one in the office believed such foolishness, and John was allowed to continue driving cab until the hearings.

He had been charged but as yet had not been convicted. He did continue to drive, and the whole town was rooting for him. The people who knew John respected him, and they would never believe it. The taxi company was booming. Women had no problem driving with him. And the rooming house—well, that's another story.

CHAPTER 11

Court day. John retained a lawyer from town. He kept telling John, "Don't worry so much. There's no way you will be found guilty." The regular judge was brought in. We figured he was somewhere around eighty or older. Once in a while, he would close his eyes as if sleeping. We sure found this odd. Once witnesses were called and the hearing was over, we held our breath. Guilty! John was found guilty on one charge and not guilty on the other two. Everyone sat stunned, especially John's lawyer. He was sentenced to probation and had to pay a fine of $1,000 to the foundation of abused women. John's lawyer turned to John and said, "This is not right. We are going to take this case to high court." We drove to Toronto (which was two and a half hours) and met with a high court lawyer. John paid him $5,000, and we came back home. John never received a bill from his previous lawyer. He told John, "I can't charge an innocent man, and I will waive all fees."

What was on the front page of the local newspaper? "Taxicab owner found guilty." John was still allowed to drive as the case was, as yet, not over. The case was in the hands of the high court.

Six months later, John received a phone call from the lawyer in Toronto. The case was thrown out because of the arresting officer's comments. "I know you're not guilty, John, but I have to arrest you in order to get that woman off my back." All three judges read no further than that.

Do you think the local paper had anything to print that week? Not that John was found "not guilty." That wouldn't have been news. Shortly after this all took place, we heard of three cases where a woman was upset over some stupid thing and charged their mates. When I hear about these cases, I think hard and long about it.

How do you spell relief? *Relief!* Although John was not guilty, he was having a hard time with the whole thing.

One evening while watching TV, John said out of the blue, "I have to talk to someone. I don't know if I'm coming or going." He needed someone who would understand. "I'm going over to church and talk to the pastor."

This church was an evangelistic church. They really care for others; he will get help there. The pastor will listen to John, pray with him, and really let John know the church is standing with him. So I thought! John was back in about thirty minutes.

"What happened? Did the pastor pray for you? Was he understanding?"

"No," John said. "He didn't have time." I was puzzled.

"What do you mean he didn't have time? It's 3:00 p.m.! Church starts at 7:00 p.m. He has four hours."

John sat down in his recliner. "It seems as though he's going on a four-day golf trip and has to get ready. He told me to phone the assistant pastor. I did! He doesn't have time either. His wife is going grocery shopping, and he had to babysit."

I was shocked! The shepherd of the sheep is too busy to tend his flock because he's going golfing. No wonder no one goes to church anymore. At six thirty, John was still in his chair.

"Aren't you going to get ready for church? It's Wednesday night. Time for prayer meeting!" He didn't go, and John never entered the church again, ever. John continued to drive four or five days a week. Most of the time, he sat in his chair at home. He wouldn't go out to eat, although he had a few favorite restaurants. He wouldn't drive to the casino anymore. He wouldn't budge.

CHAPTER 12

John was now sixty-eight years old. It was 2006. I asked John if he was even interested in the company anymore. He said no, he wasn't. He wanted to sell the company, and that was fine with me. I was sixty-four by now and had the income from the rooming house. The bills were all paid by that money. He had his old-age pension and would have no bills to pay. He would be okay. One of the drivers wanted to buy the company, and John sold it to him.

By now, John was losing weight. His recliner was his home base. He got out of it to use the bathroom or open a can of soup. He didn't want to talk anymore, not just to me, to anyone. Sometimes one of the drivers would stop by for a visit. They talked; he nodded his head. I often wondered what he was thinking about all day, so one day, I asked him, "John, when you're sitting here all day, what do you think about?"

He didn't hesitate. "I've been proven not guilty! What about the pastors at the church? Are they guilty of anything? Or are they not guilty?"

I tried my best to tell him that we don't have to give an account to God for anyone else and what they do. We need to try and forgive others. They have to live their lives the best they know how; we need to worry about how we live ours. "How many times had the pastor been by to ask me why I don't go to church anymore? Right! They're too busy?"

One day, he got up out of his chair and said, "I'm going fishing!" And he headed toward his van. I opened the house door and asked him, "Don't you need a fishing rod?"

"No!" he yelled back. Three hours later he was back.

"Did you catch anything?"

"No, they weren't biting!" I thought this to be odd as he had no fishing rod or bait with him.

A few weeks later, I saw him holding up both hands up high and moving them about. It looked as if he was trying to put the thread through the needle. This went on for about ten minutes, then stop, then start again.

On one occasion, he asked a tenant to go with him to do a job. About thirty minutes later, the tenant was back, alone. I asked where John was.

"He parked in the middle of the road in front of Shopper's Drug Mart. All the drivers are honking their horns, trying to get him to move. They're all yelling at him. For some reason, he's holding a $20 bill in his hand. He is waiting for his doctor to come by as he owes for a bill."

I got in my car and drove as fast as I dared. There he was sitting in his van in the middle of the road. I parked and walked over to his window, which was down.

"John, what are you doing?"

"I'm waiting for our doctor to pay $20, and I'm not moving until the bill is paid."

My heart sank! I worked in the nursing homes long enough to know what was happening.

I asked, "Could I take the $20 bill and pay her?" That was fine with him.

"Are you okay to drive home? Want me to drive?" That was okay with him also. He got out and went to the passenger side door and got in. I asked him what bill he owed the doctor.

"It's for the soup. She buys me soup."

I phoned our doctor and explained. "Don't let him drive, hide his keys and bring him to the office the next day." She was shocked to see how much weight he had lost in such a short time. She asked what he was eating.

"Soup, I like soup," John said. I explained that he refused to eat at all unless I heated soup for him. He went for tests, and just as

I suspected, his mind was going downhill fast. I looked after him at home and went to the casino at night. I couldn't stay away from the place. A tenant looked in on him often. John thought his recliner was his bed and slept there day and night. It was like pulling teeth to get him to have a shower.

We were watching TV one evening when he claimed to have pains in his chest. He almost doubled over, and I quickly called 911. He had a heart attack.

Over the months, he got worse and had to be admitted to the geriatrics ward in the hospital. I would visit often. One evening, the nurse told me to be careful when I went in his room.

"John saw an army brigade passing through his room." We both smiled at that. Sometimes he knew me, sometimes not. A couple times, he asked if I had seen Anne. I told him, "Yes, I see Anne quite often." I began to wonder why I even went to visit him. He often asked who I was. He just didn't know me.

While in the hospital, he had a massive heart attack. He was holding on when I visited him later. I went to the casino and spent most of the evening there. I took advantage of the free buffet. I returned home around 10:00 p.m. I was settling in to watch TV for a while when the phone rang. I was told to come quickly, or it may be too late. By the time I got to the hospital, he had another heart attack. When I walked in, the nurse met me and said, "I'm sorry, he's gone." I went to the side of his bed and hardly recognized him.

John was buried on December 18, 2006. I often told John that if we kept going the way we were going, we might not live to see our twentieth wedding anniversary. We missed it by four days.

CHAPTER 13

(Names have been changed to protect their identities.)

I was alone now. After selling the taxi company and having no one to talk to, he didn't have the will to live. I didn't know how I felt. Sad, certainly! And as sad as it sounds, I felt relief. I wouldn't have to chase after him any longer to make his wrongs, right? What are the odds that square in the middle of a residential area, there was a house for sale, a duplex? And we bought it. What are the odds that he knew I would need a good income after he was gone? I would have no worries now and was so grateful for it. There was no doubt in my mind that he loved me. I knew he did. But the wrong was always there for me. What will he do next? I never knew. I guess that's why I felt relieved. That chapter in my life was over. Did I love John? How do you love someone you don't respect? Constant lies, always on edge, that seemed to be my life. I have to say, I guess I loved him; at times, I just don't know.

Now a new chapter starts, I'm free with nothing to do. The tenants in the back were behaving, sort of. A few of the tenants got up, had a beer for breakfast, and would continue until they passed out around 6:00 or 7:00 p.m.

It was relatively quiet. The one good thing about it was they always paid their rent. I guess that was better than sleeping under the bridge. The ones on disability usually had the government send their checks directly to me. Many couldn't work because they either had drug or alcohol problems. That was no problem for them. They were given social assistance and had enough left for their necessities, such as smokes, scratch tickets, or beer. It was never a problem for some of the guys to drink twelve or even eighteen beers in a day. It was annoying to me that they seldom ate. Now I was at my home away from home just about every day. It was such a draw. I had no one to answer to and had no friends.

One afternoon, as I sat in my living room, I thought of something that I needed to buy. I drove to the mall, but when I got there, I couldn't remember what I needed. I drove along the front of the stores but just couldn't bring the thing to mind. As I was leaving to go back home, I saw a man standing by the grocery store with three or four bags by his side. He had been a good customer of ours when we had the taxi company. I pulled over and asked if he needed a ride. He yelled back that he had called a cab but had been waiting for over forty-five minutes. He told me to wait a minute. He called the cab stand and cancelled the trip. He jumped in with me. I drove him home, and he took out a $5 bill and handed it to me. I pushed his hand away and said, "I don't want that. I'm glad I could give you a lift." He insisted that I take it and a cab would have cost him twice that amount. He left the $5 bill on the seat.

Back at home, the phone rang. It was the same guy. He wanted to know what I was doing these days for excitement. I told him, "Not much. Just hanging out." I didn't mention the gambling. He asked me, "Now that you don't have the taxi company any longer, do you still drive people?"

I told him, "No, I don't."

"If I give you $10, will you drive me to work?" He worked around fifteen kilometers outside of town at a resort. I told him yes, I would drive him, but he didn't need to pay me. I drove him to the resort, and he gave me $10. I'll call him Don.

"Can you pick me up at 10:00 p.m. and drive me home?" I did pick him up. On the way to his house, he asked if I could drive him every day. He mentioned that I had just saved him $16. The cab fares were $18 each way. He would be happy to pay $20 for the two trips each day. It would save him $80 a week. Don was a server and made good tips, two to three hundred a night. I told him I would think about it. I gave it five minutes of thought that evening and decided if he wanted to give me $20 a day, I'd take it. After all, I had just made $25 for doing what I enjoy—driving.

When I picked him up the next day, he asked, "Can I give your number to the other workers?" They wanted to get in on a good deal. It didn't take long for my number to get around. Most of the people worked different shifts, so there were many trips a day. I was busy from morning until night. I was making hundreds of dollars just by doing what I loved doing.

It didn't take long for the taxi companies to get wind of what was going on. The owner of one company had a lawyer write me a letter and tell me to stop driving people, and stop immediately. I wrote back and told him I had no intention of stopping. "If people hand me five or ten dollars from time to time, what is that to you?" I also asked the lawyer, "If people wanted to give you money, wouldn't you take it?" I never heard back! The other taxi company went to the town hall. They said, "You (town hall) should stop her from taking our business away." The owner was asked if he had ever seen anyone give me money. He said he hadn't seen that happen. The town hall wanted the owner to bring in proof. I guess it's a true saying: what you *think* you know is not actually *what* you know.

CHAPTER 14

I had money from the rooming house, from driving, Canada Pension, and old-age security. Driving and gambling. That was my life. Did God fit in somewhere? I thought of His goodness from time to time. I had everything! Not much time for anything or anyone else.

I believe I have met every personality that exists on the planet. I wondered some days how much longer I can cope listening to these people, everyone with a different story. One of the boys from the rooming house wanted me to drive him to a friend's house. He asked me to wait for him. He was just going to say hello—it would only take a minute. It took me a while to catch on. I mentioned it to Don, and he said, "Are you crazy? He's picking up drugs. That's why it only takes a minute." I soon learned there were seven drug houses in town. At least they were the ones I took people to. I made so many trips to the beer and liquor stores. I could drive there with my eyes closed. I would sit and wait for these people and think, *What a waste of humanity*. Alcohol and drugs, what a waste. At one time, I had seven men and women at the rooming house. All the guys were between forty-seven and sixty-two. None had ever been married. The bottle was their wife.

On another occasion, Don asked me to drive him to one of his three girlfriends' apartment. He soon came out and asked if I would stop off at the liquor store. That finished, he asked if I could take him to girlfriend no. 2. He wasn't gone long and jumped in the car, cursing a blue streak. I told him to stop it; there's no reason to be cursing Jesus like that. You made your life the way it is, not God.

"Yeah, sorry, you're right. Quite a life I'm living, eh?"

We discussed the fact that he didn't have to live life like this. It was his own choice.

"Guess you're right, as usual, but what else is there to life? I've got my women, drugs, and liquor. Couldn't ask for much more!"

We finally made it home, and I was glad to see the end of him for a while. While I'm sitting in the parking lot, he came back to the car and knocked on the window. I put the window down, "Did you forget something, Don?"

"You see, it's like this. My girlfriend wants to have a threesome, and I can't find another woman. I don't suppose you'd be interested, would you?"

Now here's my question. How many times in life would you get a generous offer like that? Boy, is he drunk! I told him I was very sorry to have to decline his offer. He went in with the forty-ounce bottle of vodka and passed out after a couple of hours.

Most of the people I drove were men. But…I did drive Louise. She also worked at the resort as a server. After her shift was over at 10:00 p.m., she would change out of her uniform into regular clothes. She would then sit at the bar and drink. I often wondered why the resort would allow this. She would call me after a couple of hours, and I would drive her home. Many times I helped get her to her door. On one occasion, she was doing her grocery shopping. She was usually mad at her husband for one reason or another. Today was no exception. On the way to pick her up, I told myself to count how many times she used a very filthy word. This was her every-day language. It was a fifteen-minute drive to her house. She got in, slammed the door, and started. I began to count, one, two, three, fifteen, twenty-seven, fifty-five, sixty-seven, seventy-four. I have no idea what she talked about. I mentioned that the next time I drive her, could she lose one particular word. I didn't really mind driving people, but the cursing was getting to me. They never heard me curse God. In fact, they all knew that I loved God. Many times while driving, religion would come up.

One lady told me, "Oh yes, I read the Bible every day!"

I asked one guy if he believed in heaven and hell. "I don't really know and don't care. I'm Roman Catholic and don't need to worry about such stupid things." I tried to explain that it didn't matter what church you go to; it's a personal matter. Each person will have to give an account for their actions.

> But for those who are self seeking and who reject Christ and follow evil there will be wrath and anger. But heaven awaits those who trust Christ. (Romans 2:6–11)

> So that, having been justified by His grace we might become heirs, having the hope of eternal life. (Titus 3:7)

He leaned forward and looked at me. "Don't tell me you actually believe that crap?" I assured him that I do indeed believe in heaven and that there is a hell. The Bible is God's road map for our life, and the way is made very clear. I believe every word in the Bible is true. He shook his hand as if to say "Just keep driving." After a couple of minutes, he told me, "You believe what you want. I'll take my chances."

Many times I drove Trudy. Town people called her an "out-and-out drunk." I must say I could see where that was coming from. She, too, worked at the resort out of town, so we used to have long talks when she was sober. Her shift started at 4:00 p.m. and finished between 10:00 p.m. and 11:00 p.m. Most days when I picked her up to take her to work, she smelled of alcohol. I asked if she had been drinking!

"No! No! No! I'm on my way to work, I can't drink." I got her to work, and most days, I watched as she took one step straight and two steps sideways. She always made it inside. I wondered why the manager let her work her shift. One day sticks out in my mind worse than others. I was parked on the street waiting for her. She was holding onto the side of the building unable to get to the car. She finally made it and flung the door open. She fell in and half smiled.

"How the —— are you, girl? I'm doing okay in this country, rev this thing up, and get me to work?" I started on our way. She was so drunk.

"You can't go to work in this condition, Trudy. You'll be fired!" She threw her arms up in the air and laughed so hard.

"I won't be fired. They need me. They can't get any help. I'm the only server on tonight."

When we arrived at the resort, she opened the door and fell out.

"Oops! I lost my step." Again, she stumbled inside, and yes, she completed her shift.

So many times I tried to talk to her. I just had to know why she had to be drunk twenty-four hours a day. What was so bad in her life? My heart was aching for her. She was generous in her own way. Every day on the way to her work, she would stop at a store and always ask if I would like something. I'd say no. That didn't matter; she always bought me some little thing. I found there was no sense to even try to talk to her as she was never sober.

On the way to work, the boys would stop at Tim Hortons for their coffee. They soon learned I liked double chocolate doughnuts. I ate so many double chocolate doughnuts over the years it's a wonder I didn't smell like chocolate.

The very worst time in this whole driving business was one winter morning. I was sound asleep. The phone rang! Looking at the clock, I saw that the time was 1:20 a.m. I answered the phone. It was Louise. She had a (few) drinks at the bar and lost track of time.

I asked, "Have you looked outside?" Meaning the snow that was coming down and piling up. She lived out in the country, and I didn't think I could drive her.

"Anna banana, get the —— out here and get me home, girl." I got dressed and looking out the window one more time, all the time thinking there's no way I can drive in this. The snow plough would not come until the storm let up. There was already about ten inches on the ground and more coming. No track had been made. I made it to my car. The temperature was -21°C. I made it to the highway. A few vehicles had made one lane, so I kept in it. Somehow, I made it to the resort. She got in.

"How the ——— are you girl? Get me away from this ——— place, Annie bananie." I answered that I probably felt better than she did. She couldn't find the seatbelt, so I got her hooked up; we started heading for the country. This was not the highway. It was a two-lane country road. I listened to her ramble on about her stupid, idiotic coworkers for a few minutes. She then passed out. I grabbed the collar of her coat with my right hand and held her up as best I could. I was afraid her head would hit the side window. I drove with my left hand. The snow was pounding down now, and I had to get as close to the windshield as I could. I hoped I could somehow stay in the middle of the road. The wipers were going full blast. A thirty-minute ride took one hour, but I got her home. I didn't dare go down her driveway in fear I would never get out again. I sort of parked to one side and hoped no cars would pass. She got her seat belt off and grabbed her bags of goodies. She opened the car door and fell into the snowbank. I helped her gather her water bottles, trays of salad, and whatever else we could find. I waited until she made it to the door and went in. Now, I have to get myself back to my house. I made it, put my pajamas back on and sat in my recliner. It was warm and cozy. I sat for a while and just wondered about things. Why do people live like this? Why? Why?

I picked her up the next day for her shift. She was as sober as a judge. But wait! Tonight is coming, and the racket starts all over again.

CHAPTER 15

The years passed by. Where did they go? I'm in my seventies now. My life consisted of alcoholics, drug addicts, ex-convicts, and gambling. I would often think about my life and wonder what in the world am I doing? I'm not really living; I'm just existing. Is this all there is for me?

Every month, without fail, I would receive flyers in the mail from the many casinos I would go to. Free this and free that. Everything was free as long as you spent your hard-earned cash there. I was always excited. Which casino has the best deal? I decided to call my sister and ask her to come along. We would be going to NY just across the border from Niagara Falls, Canada. We both had passports and could come and go as many times as we wanted. It wouldn't be for a couple more weeks. The room and all meals were free. We would go on October 17 and 18, 2018.

One day after receiving my bank statements and credit card statements. I wondered how much do I owe this month? I usually didn't pay any attention to the amounts. I had two lines of credit from two different banks. One line was $18,000; the other was $13,000. One of my credit cards was limited to $19,000. I would pay a little each month and keep putting more on them. I longed to have them paid off, but that wasn't going to happen. This day, I decided to add up my gambling bills just to see how far in debt I really was. I was shocked but glad it wasn't more. Just $38,000. I would say that over the years, I probably wasted $250,000, if not more.

So addicted! One evening, I decided to leave all my cards at home. I took $1,000 cash, and when that was gone, I'd come home.

At least that's what I told myself. It didn't take long to lose that. I can't describe how I felt. I think I was at the lowest point in my life. I felt angry at God. He knows which machine I should play. Why doesn't he show me? Not only did I blame myself, now I was blaming God.

These machines are not going to beat me. I'll drive home (one hour) and grab my credit cards and return. I would teach these slot machines a lesson. It was 10:00 p.m. by the time I got my cards and returned to the casino. I played the limit I was allowed for the day! It's 5:00 a.m. Where could I get my hands on more money? I couldn't, not today! I sat on the stool and stared at the machine. I'm glad I didn't have a hammer. I don't even have $2 to tip the valet. How shameful! While waiting outside for my car to be brought to me, I had many thoughts. I was so depressed. My first thought was, *Why not just drive your car into the rock cut and kill yourself?* No one will know what happened. Or better still, you have a bottle of Tylenol 3s, why not just take the whole bottle and sit in your chair; someone will find you.

As I was waiting for my car, I heard a soft voice say. "Write the book!" Where did that come from? What book? I got in my car and drove home. Safely!

CHAPTER 16

I phoned and made reservations for the NY casino. We arrived at 2:00 p.m. and checked in. I went directly to the gaming floor, and my sister went to the room with our overnight bags. We were going to meet for supper at five thirty. Free buffet, of course. I had given her US $200. She said she had only spent $20 so far. I didn't tell her how much I had gone through already. At the casino, you could win a little. That was always a plus. After playing for about nine hours, I bought a hot dog and pop and went to our room.

My sister was reading. She looked up and asked how I was doing. I said, "Okay, you know, win some, lose some." The next day, October 18, I went to the floor to play and stayed until 2:00 pm. I was out of money. No problem, I brought all my cards with me. I took out US $500 but had a Canadian credit card. It cost me much more than $500. We met for supper. She played a bit and went back to our room. I took out another $500, then $300. When that was gone, I just sat and watched as people put in twenties and fifties into the machines. What in the world am I doing? Am I stupid all together? The lights flashing, the bells ringing, the bright-colored emblems on the machines, I loved it. I should quit this foolishness, but I couldn't. As you read, you may be thinking, all she had to do was stop going; just quit. You can tell an alcoholic or a drug addict to just stop, just quit, but you might get a slap in the head. It's not that easy. An addiction can't be stopped that easy. I had spent well over $3,000 and had $100 bill in my pocket. I know this $100 will give me a jackpot, but which machine? I remembered a machine that I had won $400 on. I made my way over to it.

An oriental lady was playing. I waited until she left then grabbed the machine. I didn't want anyone else to sit there. I put the $100 bill in the machine and hit the button. I wanted the money to last awhile so wasn't playing maximum like I usually did. After a few spins, I began to cough. Mild at first but it was getting worse. It became a deep, hacking cough. I couldn't stop. People were looking at me as they walked by. I had to leave the casino. I hit the button and cashed out what I had left of the $100 and put the tab in my pocket. The hacking was constant every few seconds. I made it to our room, and as soon as I walked in, my sister asked, "What is wrong with you? Are you okay? What's going on?"

I didn't know. The only thing I knew was whoever was playing that machine must have had an infection and now I have it. COVID-19 was as yet unheard of. Somehow, I made it through the night; neither one of us slept. I have asthma and kept using my puffers, but they didn't help. I have always been healthy otherwise and seldom was sick. We had a four-and-a-half-hour drive ahead of us. My sister cashed the tab on the way out. I made it to the valet, and we started on our way. My sister drove, and I held napkins over my mouth while hacking all the way. I can only remember one thing. I will never go to another casino again in my life. I told my sister, and she said a bit sarcastically "Oh yeah, right, I guess so!" She had no idea how serious I was. I made it home somehow and stopped at the drugstore for cough medicine. So many kinds! I settled on one. It was supposed to stop the coughing in its tracks. Nothing was stopping this. Over the next few days, I tried six or seven different kinds, but nothing worked.

I removed my jacket and shoes and fell into bed. Laying down was worse. I was cold, sweating, head aching, and just plain miserable. I was able to drive a few times but wore a mask because of the cough. I sure didn't want anyone else to catch whatever it was I had. When it got worse and I started throwing up, I couldn't drive any longer. It seemed better when I sat up. But I was tired, sick, and tired. I hoped that when I went to bed, sleep would come. I was coughing only every twenty minutes or so now. Maybe I'm getting better. One night as I was trying to sleep and facing the wall, a strange thing happened. I heard that voice again.

"Could I have my old job back?" I was sure someone was in my bedroom. I was puzzled; what does that mean, have your old job back? The voice was quiet and soothing.

"It's like this! I created the universe and used to be in charge of that until you took over. I don't have much to do these days. You have kind of made a mess of your life, why not let me have my old job back? You put your complete faith in me, and we'll see what happens."

I laughed! I wasn't laughing at God. It was because of such a profound statement. I had some thinking to do. My thoughts were racing a mile a minute. God loves me! He has the answers. All I have to do is put my complete trust in Him. I knew it wouldn't be easy. After trusting myself all these years and not doing so well, it was time. My life is a complete mess.

The rooming house is unsellable. No one has that kind of cash just laying around. I'm stuck. I didn't want to die in this rooming house. I wanted peace in my life for a while. I'm so tired; in fact, I was beyond tired. My dream of going home out east would never happen, so I thought.

I knew the Bible well enough to know of the many miracles God had performed in the past; and the Bible also says that God is the same, yesterday, today and will be the same, always, forever. My mind was made up. The games I had been playing with God were going to stop. I either trust Him, or I don't. It's up to me. My complete trust was going to be in Him. I've come to the end of the line. I couldn't see a way out, but I didn't have to. God wanted to and would lead me step by step. I was going to do what I thought was right. If I go off track, God will get me back on. The first and biggest hurdle was to stop gambling, to never set my feet ever again inside a casino. Then the thoughts came, fast and furious. The main one being, "What will you do with all your spare time? How will you fill your evenings? What about that jackpot you try so hard to win? You'll be upset if you hear about someone else winning it."

I could always read my Bible in the evenings. After all, the Bible holds a plan to set people free. The Bible is a road map for the rest of my life, and I'm determined to follow it. I needed freedom from this madness, and there was only one way to get it.

> But seek first His kingdom and His righteousness and all these things will be given to you. (Matthew 6:33)

> So I say to you: Ask and it will be given, seek and you will find; knock and the door will be opened to you. (Luke 11:9)

> For everyone looks out for their own interests. (Philippians 2:21)

That was going to change and change in a hurry. "Set your hearts on things above where Christ is, seated at the right hand of God. Set your minds on things above and not on earthly things" (Colossians 3:1).

While sitting in my chair, I prayed. I talked to God, and I knew He heard me. I needed Him and told Him so. I asked for forgiveness for the life I had wasted. I can't go back and live my life over, but I can start to live a meaningful life from this day going forward. My old life didn't matter anymore. Each day was starting in prayer, in thankfulness. I wanted the spirit of God to lead me each step of the way. Some days I needed God, but most days, not. Now I had finally surrendered. My trust was being put in Him. Whatever came my way, He would help me get through it. I couldn't see what was in my future, but one thing I knew, my old life was gone. God's love is deeper than the ocean and higher than the sky. I was going to take advantage of that. My life was going to be lived by faith. I couldn't see God. I couldn't touch God, but I knew without a doubt, He was there with me. It didn't matter how I had lived. What was more important was how I was going to live.

CHAPTER 17

Now I was amazed every time I read the Bible. I had studied the Bible for years and had gone to three Bible colleges. I never saw that it was possible to have a good peaceful and fulfilling life. Now I know God has a good life ahead for me.

Jeremiah 33:3 says, "Call to me and I will show you great and mighty things." I held onto that. I'll do my part, whatever it may be. I'll work hard and believe.

My desire for gambling was gone. That was always a mystery to me. How can I be so addicted to gambling, and the next day, the desire was completely gone. I sometimes would think of the flashing lights, the slot machines, and the hustle and bustle. The excitement I felt when I won ten or twenty dollars was now gone. The free buffets, the free hotel rooms, the free parking, gone. When I think about it now, I think "free"; they sure weren't free. Sometimes they cost me thousands of dollars a day. I knew I would never step inside another casino again. I guess God had to get my attention and He sure did. Those thirty-two days of sickness was enough to wake me up. People who knew I went to the casino (sometimes) would say to me, "I hope God has lots of slot machines in heaven." I thought it was a stupid thing to say but realized it was said in ignorance and let it pass.

I wrote out a scripture one day and put it on the side of my table. Whenever I sat down, it was staring at me: "So do not fear, I am with you; do not be dismayed, for I am your God. I will strengthen you and help you; I will uphold you with my righteous right hand" (Isaiah 41:10). Isaiah 41:13 says, "For I am your God who takes hold of your right hand and says to you, do not fear. I will help you." I memorized those two scriptures and said them over and over.

Finally after thirty-two days, I felt better. I could drive again. The boys didn't phone often. I guessed they had found other rides. One day while sitting and thanking God, the phone rang. It was Mike. He said he needed to go to Walmart, and his $5 bill was calling my name. He got in and looked at me. "You're not hacking your lungs out. Are you okay now?" I assured him I was fine. He got out to shop at Walmart and asked me to wait. He would only be a few minutes. He handed me the $5 bill. I was holding the bill and thinking for the first time this $5 isn't going into a slot machine. While sitting and waiting for Mile, I heard that ever-so-soft voice again. It was not loud, but I heard it.

"What are you holding in your hand?" I announced that it was a $5 bill. Again, I heard "What are you sitting in?" I again answered, "I'm sitting in my old, rusted-out bucket of a car." For the third time, the voice. "This $5 bill and this car are going to pay off the $38,000 you have in gambling debts." I now have sense enough to believe. Sort of! How many $5 bills is it going to take and how many years do I have to drive in order to pay off that amount of money. Mike came out of Walmart and got in. "You still holding that $5 bill?"

"Yes" I told him. "This bill is a miracle working bill. It's going to pay all my debts."

"Oh, okay! I just have one more stop, then you can drive me home." I did take him home and now that $5 bill is $10. The people soon started calling me again for rides. The money I was now making was going into a box. I had written on the box "Gambling debt, $38,000." After one month, I had $1,200 in it. I could hardly believe it. It was years since I had that much money and no casino to go to. I felt like shouting. I kept these things to myself and pondered the goodness of God. Together, God and I had a good thing going, and I was not going to blow it.

Proverbs 3:5, 6 says, "Trust in the Lord with all your heart and lean not on your own understanding. In all ways, acknowledge Him and He will make your paths straight."

I drove January and February 2019 and then had to stop. A worldwide pandemic was taking place. It was a thing called COVID-19. Restaurants closed, bars closed, everything closed, except beer and liquor stores. They were essential according to the government. I could just image the riots if they couldn't get their beer. Getting drugs was no problem. They just went to the house down the street. I didn't feel comfortable driving people to the beer and liquor stores but was somewhat comforted when I read the scripture in Proverbs 13:22, "A sinner's wealth is stored up for the righteous." I didn't know if I was righteous, but I been made right with God. I continued to drive them. I had a job to do and was going to do it. If they wanted to give me $5 because they needed liquor, then my box would soon be full.

I believe it was early 2019 when we first heard of COVID in Canada. There wasn't much for me to do now. I drove from time to time to the stores, drugstores, and grocery. I stopped the drives to the drug houses. Alcohol was legal; drugs were not.

All the driving was getting to me. Listening to the people depressed me. Some days, I wanted to scream, "Sober up, stop cursing God, get a job!" I would go home sometimes and shake my head. I wanted to stop driving them. I longed often to go home, not the place where I was living, but the home I left when I was eighteen, my Nova Scotia home. I longed to have a little house near the ocean. All I needed was a little piece of land for a vegetable garden, maybe even a few chickens. Day after day, I longed for it. One day, while praying, I asked God if it was even possible. Then I remembered "All things are possible to those who believe!" (Matthew 19:26). I held onto that! I owned this rooming house, and it was not possible to sell it. I had listed it three times already. People were interested and wanted to buy it for the income. They would go to the mortgage lenders and always be told, "No, we don't give mortgages for rooming houses." It was frustrating. What was I supposed to do? I was stuck!

For a time, I had hired a man as manager. I would pay him, and he would do what I needed to be done. I would save, but that wouldn't give me enough money for a down payment on my little house in Nova Scotia.

Things were going quite well except whenever he had a fight with his married girlfriend (with five kids), he would go to Jack Daniel's (liquor) for comfort. The drinking bouts would usually last three to four days. It was kind of funny to all the other tenants because they knew when he finally sobered up and come out of his room, he always had the same explanation.

"I had a bad cold and was in bed three or four days." I feared there might be a fire or someone might fall downstairs or something. This arrangement ended.

CHAPTER 18

Things with the COVID-19 were getting better now, and I was soon back to driving guys and girls. Money was coming in again. I think God cares about the small things as well as the big things in our lives.

I started driving early in the morning and didn't have time for breakfast. I just kept going. I couldn't get a break. I was driving a guy to work one day when he asked if I could stop at the mall. He wanted to go into the dollar store. I was hungry. I had been driving all day, and it was now 3:30 p.m. As I waited for him to return, I noticed a car coming fast and right toward me. I was sure the driver was going to smash into my car. I held my breath. An elderly lady pulled up next to my car and motioned for me to roll down my car window. She was holding a small bag. I asked if she was all right.

"Oh yes, dear, my sister invited me to go for coffee. She insisted on buying me a snack, maybe a doughnut. I told her I didn't eat doughnuts. She bought it for me anyway, so I brought it with me. Would you like to have it?" I didn't know this lady! She held the bag out of her window, and I reached for it. She rolled up her window and was gone. I opened the Tim Horton's bag and almost fell over. It was a double chocolate doughnut. I was enjoying my doughnut when the guy came back.

"Where did you get that doughnut? I was only gone two or three minutes."

"You wouldn't believe me if I told you."

"Well, you could try me. I might believe you."

I had my last bite as I licked my fingers.

"The Lord gave it to me!" I heard no reply.

My cash box was getting full. Every month I would deposit what I had made along with the rooming house money. I had saved almost enough to pay off the $38,000. I had hoped to pay it off by December 31, 2019, but was short. I worked one more month and on January 31, 2020, the bills were paid—in full. I went to my car and cried. How long I cried, I can't remember. I thanked God over and over. What a difference a few months make. What a difference it makes to trust God. I had to put up with cursing, lying, and drunk or drugged people; but I made it. I never thought this day would ever come. I looked down at my bank book and slowly opened it. The book read $8.73. I had $8.73, and it was mine. I didn't owe a cent to the banks on credit cards. I could never have guessed how that small amount would grow. My steps were lighter now. The heavy load had been lifted. Now I didn't have to drive anymore; I could finally relax. But wait a minute, not so fast. God had other plans and let me know it in no uncertain terms. My driving days were certainly not over. I had come through the sickness where God had finally gotten my attention, but I still had a few more kinks to work out. I started paying 10 percent of my money to God that I owed. It was tough at first, but I soon learned the more I gave, the more I had. I watched the Christian networks as often as I could, especially on Sundays. I wasn't so sure about sending money to TV evangelists, but two programs stood out to me. They were International Fellowship of Christians and Jesus and C4I, Christians for Israel. I prayed about it and a few days later got my answer.

As I watched a program on TV, the minister quoted a scripture from Genesis 12:3, "I will bless those who bless you (Israel) and I will curse those who curse you." I felt good about these two charities, and that is where my 10 percent was going. Most important to me was the fact that they supported Holocaust survivors by feeding, clothing, and providing shelter for them. That is where my heart was drawn. I figure if those precious people could survive the prison camps for years, then I could at least help them enjoy the rest of their lives. Even though it wasn't a great amount of money that I was sending, I was honoring God by helping His people. Some of the last words Jesus spoke before He was crucified were "Feed my people," meaning the Jewish people. It was an honor for me to do this, and still today, that is where my money goes.

CHAPTER 19

While driving a young man to work one day, he asked to stop first at the beer store as per usual. On the way I asked, "How do you feel about God? Do you believe there is a God?"

He was never eager to discuss religious matters. He just laughed and said, "It's like this. You keep your God whoever He is, and I'll keep mine." I replied that the God I knew is the creator of the universe. I knew he was uncomfortable but asked anyway. "Do you mind to tell me who your god is?"

"Oh, that's simple. My god is beer." I dropped him at work and went home. I had such an uneasy feeling. A scripture I remembered reading was Galatians 6:7, "Do not be deceived: God will not be mocked. A man reaps what he sows."

I knew beforehand that I had to pick him up the next morning. That evening, his friend would drive him home. The next morning, I was parked in his driveway waiting for him. His landlady came out and said he wouldn't need a ride today. Last night he was rushed by air ambulance to Sunny Brook Hospital in Toronto. She wasn't sure he would live. I asked, "What happened to him?" She wasn't sure; she just she heard a tree had fallen on him at work.

How could a tree have fallen on him? He was a server at a resort. I later found out that he was serving customers on the patio. It was a nice evening, and the patio was full. He had just taken an order from a couple and was heading back inside to place their order. A great wind suddenly came up and a large branch of a tree broke off. It came straight toward him, and before he could get out of the way, the branch hit him square in the face. His nose was torn off and lay against his face. Splinters were imbedded in his entire face, and he lay unconscious. The wind ceased, and no one else even felt it. He was in the hospital for months as he had no memory and couldn't speak. After about eight months, he was back home. He was not able to work, so I didn't see him. He soon was able to walk and talk again. I passed him on the street one day and yelled out, "Hello, how you doing?" He pointed to his backpack. Inside were his usual six beer—his god.

I continued driving all through 2020. The money was growing, and I just put it in the bank. I'm still longing to go home. I'm sick of people with addictions. I soon had pity for these people and realized that I, too, was addicted. Only, theirs was in the open to see, mine was a hidden addiction. I guess I would have to say the worse part was listening to the cursing of God. It was everyday language to them. It was a lifestyle.

I still drive the girl that fell out of my car at work because she was so drunk. I was parked on the street one day, waiting for her to come out of the rooming house. She came walking up the driveway as straight as an arrow. She didn't stagger or even have to hold onto things. She was stone sober. I must have looked puzzled. She threw her arms up in the air and yelled, "I quit drinking! It's been two weeks now."

"You quit drinking! Did your boss make you quit?"

She said no; she was sick of herself, sick of the booze and sick of never having any money. "I work hard. I've always worked hard and don't have one red cent to my name. Guess it was time to quit." As I write, she has been sober over a year.

CHAPTER 20

There was an older black gentleman living in the rooming house. He had been there for a few years and kept mostly to himself. Of course he was an alcoholic and also addicted to scratch tickets. One day, he asked if I was still interested in selling the place. I told him of course, but people can't get a mortgage. They would have to have cash. He asked if it would be okay if he gave my number to his son. Of course, what's the harm? A few weeks later, the son called. He was coming to town to visit his dad and asked if we could discuss the rooming house. I said it would be fine but knew it would be a waste of time. I had already made up my mind that I would have this business for the rest of my life. But I know God loved me, and it was all right.

The first thing I said to him was, "I hope you have the money for the rooming house because you'll never get a mortgage from the bank." He shook his head up and down.

"You leave the money part to me, let's discuss price."

I told him I expected to get $400,000. He wanted to know if that included all the furnishing.

I told him, "Yes, if you buy this place, you can even have the tenants. I'll throw them in for free." He had to talk to some people he knew. He would get back to me. This was early 2021. I turned seventy-nine that year in April.

In the meantime back in October 2020, one of my tenants decided that he should act out. He was on a mental disability and was a psychopath. His drug of choice was marijuana, but any drug would do if he could get his hands on them. He drank six to twelve bottles of beer a day along with the drugs. The government paid his rent directly to me the rest of the money went to him. When he ran out of money for his prescriptions, the social worker just sent him another check. He needed more powerful drugs and could get them in town anywhere. After taking them, he would go ballistic. His favorite thing to do was walk up and down the halls, hour after hour, screaming and cursing. He was, however, kept somewhat in check by a bodybuilder tenant who lived below him. The screaming guy was scared of him and would quiet down after being talked to by the strong guy. After months of this the bodybuilder had enough and to my (and the other tenants') dismay, he was moving out. He needed some peace. The music thumped all night and directly over his head. How can you sleep with that going on? The guy did move out, and I knew we were all in big trouble. The favorite time of day for the screamer was 10:00 p.m. until 7:00 a.m., then he would sleep all day. The very day the bodybuilder moved out was not a good day for me. I was walking toward my own car when I heard a familiar voice behind me.

"Hey, you, you ———, I have something to say to you."

I opened my car door to get in, but he wasn't finished.

"I just wanted to let you know that now Mr. Hot Shot is gone, I'll be in charge around here. What I say goes, you understand that? If I tell the other tenants to jump, they better jump. And that goes for you too."

I was a bit surprised at such a stupid statement. But then again, I quickly considered the source.

"Okay, but starting this month, you will have to pay all the bills. There's the water bill, hydro, property taxes, and insurance as well."

He came close to my face.

"You think you're funny don't you, ———? Well, you'll find out how funny I can be."

I got in the car and drove away. I was not exactly happy. When I returned that evening, the tenants were so upset with me. I explained it all to them, and they settled down, somewhat.

How disappointed I was. I finally had someone interested in buying this place, and this is going on. There is no way he will even consider buying. The police would be called by me, or a tenant and they would come and knock on his door. He refused to answer them or open his door so the police left. That was that!

Christmas came (2020), and if anyone living there thought there was peace on earth, good will toward men, they were sadly mistaken. On Christmas day, he started at 11:00 p.m., and it ended at 7:00 a.m. Just like clockwork.

"I'm going to kill everyone in the —— place. I'll burn this shack to the ground." Again, the police were called in the early morning, around three. What a waste of time. They came, listened to my story, and knocked on his door. No answer! They left!

It wasn't getting any better. Now he was ordering tenants to move out because he didn't like them. They, of course, would be killed if they weren't gone by the end of the month. This is unbelievable. Something has to be done. Should I call the police? I don't think so. That would be a waste of time.

With the tenants on my back every day, I filed the papers to the Landlord and Tenant Act. After three weeks, they wrote back stating that the papers were filled out incorrectly and if I could file them again. I did! A month later, they wrote back to me. The papers were filled out incorrectly, and again asked if I could file again. No, I don't think so. From the information I provided, I guessed they didn't want anything to do with a psychopath. Now what? It's now March, and two tenants have moved out and no one else is moving in. Any wonder? Two more tenants were looking for places to rent. Soon, it would be just him and me.

On one occasion, a tenant asked (the bully) as he was called to please turn his music down. That didn't go over very well. Big mistake! The bully grabbed him by the throat and backed him into the kitchen. The tenant's head was slammed into the sink and broke the faucet. His head was bleeding. I called the police, and they came! I told them I wanted the guy charged. They told me in no uncertain terms that it had nothing to do with me. The tenant would have to lay the charges, and he wouldn't. I guess he thought the next time would be worse. So the bully was right. He is in charge, and there doesn't seem to be anything I can do about it.

Everyone stayed in their rooms. When they had to come out, they opened their doors slowly just in case he was lurking in the hallway. Another time, a young man was visiting a lady tenant and had brought his small dog with him. As he was leaving, the dog barked once. The bully didn't like that even one bit. He flew out of his room and went to the steps and yelled down, "Come up here, you ——, and I'll kill you!"

The young man asked who that guy was yelling at. But before the young man was outside, the bully pounded downstairs and grabbed him by the collar. He hit the young man square in the mouth with his fist, and the blood flew everywhere. It was on the door, the wall, and himself. The young man just stood there holding his mouth. There were two other tenants who saw this take place. A tenant called the police. Of course, they came. But why? I again said, "Look, Officer, you have to charge this guy. He's out of control."

The police asked if there were any witnesses. There were two. By this time, the young man left, and the bully retreated to his room. There was safety for him there. The police said, "We'll go up and talk to him." They returned downstairs and stated that there was no answer when they knocked on his door.

"We'll go catch up with the other guy and talk to him." A few minutes later, the police were back. They explained that the young man started the whole thing to begin with. No charges were laid. Why would I think there would be? On two occasions, the police told me to get him out of the rooming house.

"He has to be put in a place where he can be supervised. This is no place for him." What did they think I was trying to do? On another occasion, an officer told me, "Why do you keep calling us? You're wasting our time. We have better things to do than to be running up here every day." I asked to speak to the supervisor at the detachment. He would make time to see me in a few days. I explained everything (he already knew) and asked how I could get this guy out. His answer was very simple.

"I'm going deer hunting for a week. When I get back, I'll look into it further. I have a police friend on the Toronto force. I'll ask him." I never heard from him again. I guess he was busy cooking deer steaks on his barbecue.

CHAPTER 21

In the meantime, the man who was interested in buying the place knew all about the foolishness that was going on. I supposed his father kept him informed. This man had talked to the bully several times himself on behalf of his father. That made matters worse. The man came to me and said, "Don't worry about that, idiot, after I buy this place, I'll take care of him." I had tried nine different agencies for help. I spoke to my member of parliament twice. That was useless. They informed me to "Send the forms to the Landlord and Tenant Act. We'll give you the forms."

No thanks, you keep your forms and do whatever it is you do.

I went to the mental health office. Nothing they could do. I talked several times to his case worker. No, nothing she could do. I filled out forms to the courts and sent them twice. No, they had never received them. They had been faxed to the courts, but of course, they never received them. Am I having a nightmare? Will I wake up soon?

We at the rooming house were doing the best we could. Some nights, we got a few hours of sleep. All I knew was that I loved God and knew He loved me. The only thing I could do was hope and trust.

Finally, I sent a registered letter to my mayor, begging her for help. She had someone phone me, letting me know that she was sorry we were going through this. She would try to help. After a few phone calls, I was informed that my letter was given to the community police officer. They would be happy to look into the matter. What? She gave the letter to a police officer! That was the end of that. I guess he was busy. I even tried the by-law officer. No, can't help even if there is a by-law stating you must be quiet after 11:00 p.m. This was his favorite time of day, and nothing could be done? I was at the end of the road. No right turns, no left turns. It was the end!

CHAPTER 22

I phoned my sister and told her I had an offer of $360,000 for the place. It was worth a lot more.

Her exact words were, "Look, you're seventy-nine years old, Anne, take the money and run. You are always talking about going back home. Here's your chance. You will be able to live quite comfortably. You have your two pensions (old age and Canada pension), you have money in the bank, and if you sell, you can have your dream."

That was all I needed to hear. I accepted his offer. Two weeks later, the guy phoned me. "I would like to give you twenty thousand more than what I offered before." What? I was okay with the first amount, but hey, if you want to give me $20,000 more, I'll take it. That made it $380,000.

The summer wore on (2021). I kept driving, and the bully kept bullying. There was no help coming our way. The police had been called forty-eight times to date.

We settled on July 1 as the closing date. I continued to hope against hope that he could some way get the money. Two weeks before the closing date, he phoned to inform me that he was having a hard time coming up with the money. He couldn't get it from the banks. He was going to try something else. What was wrong with this guy? Hadn't I mentioned four or five times that the banks were a no-no? My heart sank! I was so excited about selling, and now I'm hearing he can't come up with the money. At least I felt excited for a while. I knew God had not forgotten about me. He would come up with something. Things will work out. Two days before the closing date, my lawyer phoned. Could I come to his office? I sure could! I sat down, and he held up a paper.

"Guess what this is?" I hoped and prayed all in a split second. Yes! It was what I hoped it would be. I sat back in my chair and couldn't say a word. July 1 was a holiday, and the banks wouldn't be open.

"It's Friday, and the check might not go through today, but I'll do my best to deposit it." It was one o'clock, Friday. The bank will close at 5:00 p.m. He has four hours to get there. I kept thinking that the check wasn't real and it might bounce.

I waited until 4:00 p.m. I couldn't wait any longer. I had to know. I went to the teller and handed her my bank book.

"Could you update my book, please?" She put the book into the machine and handed it back to me, closed. I thanked her and left the bank. I didn't dare open the book. My heart was pounding as I sat in my car. The last time I was excited about opening my bank book was back on January 31, 2020. Now it's July 2021. At that time, I had $8.73 in my account. I had to open the book. I had to know. I just stared. There was nothing to say or do. I remembered the $5 bill I received at Walmart. It certainly grew. This time, the book didn't read $8.73. I read almost half a million. I put my arms on the steering wheel then put my face in my hands and cried. *God, You did it. You really did it. Thank You!* I stayed in the parking lot for a while then went home and told the tenants the rooming house hand been sold. I apologized so many times to them. I tried, oh how I tried, to get the bully out but couldn't. I failed them.

A door flew open and out comes you-know-who.

"I heard that, ———. I hope the new owner knows who's in charge around here." Well, we will see!

It was approximately four months later when the police came and took him out in handcuffs. It wasn't made clear to me when they finally took him. The tenants heard the commotion, and all gathered to see what was going on. When they saw the two officers escorting him out, they clapped and cheered. One tenant said, "We'll be able to sleep tonight, guys!" They all said in unison, "Yes!"

The police had been called forty-eight times with no results. What in the world had changed? I guess I'll never know.

I hope no one ever asks me what I think of our town's finest boys in blue. I just might tell them.

CHAPTER 23

A few days after the sale, I went back to the bank and asked for a draft for $38,000. I was so excited to pay my 10 percent. I gave the teller a note with the name of where I wanted the money to go. She looked at the note.

"Do you know these people? Are you sure you want to send money to them?"

Yes! I was sure! I'd never been so sure of anything in my life. It was going to the International Fellowship of Christians and Jews! She went ahead with the draft. I didn't know how many Holocaust survivors would be helped with that money, but I knew a few would be. On my way home, the number $38,000 was ringing in my head. I was sure I had heard that same amount before. Of course! It was the same amount that my gambling debt was up to. I may have failed God over the years, but He did not fail me.

The next month, August, my sister and I flew to Halifax. I was in search of that little house near the ocean. By this time, I've learned to pray about everything in my life had been so busy, so hectic. I wasn't sure I could handle peace and quiet. I sure was going to give it a shot. We looked at seven houses. All were below $100,000. Some places were nightmares, and we wondered how people could even live there. The fourth one we looked at was a small two-bedroom with land enough for a garden and maybe a hen house. I liked it, but everything was brown and depressing. Brown cupboards, brown baseboards, brown trim around the doors and windows. The doors and bathroom—of course, they were brown. I couldn't get past the color. We kept looking. Time was running out. We only had three days and would have to fly back to Toronto. I told the real estate agent that I would take the last one we looked at, number 7. It was a mess, but a little elbow grease could get it in shape. The agent convinced me to go back again and look at number 4. The brown house (inside, white outside). The second time I saw the house, I looked past the brown and saw what could be. I put an offer in, and the price was settled. I signed all the papers, and we flew back to Toronto. The closing date was December 17. There was to be a three-month wait. The real estate agent phoned a month later and said I could move in on November 17, one month earlier.

I left Ontario on November 2 and stayed with my niece for two weeks. I sold my little money maker car and bought a Dodge Caravan. It was loaded to the hilt. I can't begin to say enough about my family. In the sixty-two years I had been away, family members had died; others were born. I'm getting to know them slowly, and it is a pleasure. They make me feel welcome. One family member gave me a chair. Another gave me a kitchen table and two chairs. Some gave me dishes, sheets, and you name it. My sister-in-law and niece come to dinner every Sunday. In Ontario, our meals are breakfast, dinner, and supper, but I've got the hang of it now. The house is fully painted, new flooring, a large deck, and all the furniture I need. Everyone who comes to visit only had one thing to say.

"It's so cozy." I laugh each time I hear it. No more brown cupboards or brown trim. No more brown windows.

It has been a long and nightmarish journey for me. Long and hard! I would never want to live it over. I regret the years lost in going my own way. I really messed things up, and God is longsuffering and was always with me along the journey. The world is a dark place and is only getting darker.

Since coming home, I haven't heard one curse word. No one in the family curses God that I know about.

No more phone calls at 1:20 a.m. No more trips to the drug houses or liquor store. I'm close to the ocean and can walk on the beach, go to the lighthouse, or watch the fishermen bring in their lobsters. I'm enjoying the fresh fish so much. I'm enjoying every minute of being home. My garden was filled with tomatoes and peas and cucumbers.

At times, I am overwhelmed at the goodness of God. I think God may not be finished with me yet.

In the beginning of my book, I mentioned a vision I had at the chapel while in the air force. It took sixty years of wondering what it meant. It had been made clear to me. The horse-drawn chariot is a symbol of war. The prancing horse was to be the way my life would be lived. Always facing obstacles, always a fight to survive, always struggling. The books inside the chariot, new, used, old, and tattered. They were the many lives I came in contact with over the years. Each one having a different story, a different personality. Each one with a story all their own.

I finally have the peace and quiet I longed for. I read my Bible and pray and know that I will not be interrupted. That is worth everything to me.

Years ago at the casino, God spoke to me and said, "Write the book." I didn't know what that meant then, but I do know now. I have just turned eighty and have written "the book." I thank God every day that He took my dark world and turned it into light.

Look to the Lord and His strength, seek His
face always. (Psalms 105:4)

You, Lord, are forgiving and good, abound-
ing in love to all who call on you. (Psalms 86:5)

ABOUT THE AUTHOR

She grew up in rural Nova Scotia and left at the age of eighteen. She returned to live there at the age of seventy-nine. Her life consisted of one mishap after another. Yes, she believed there was a God somewhere and even believed that He might love her. In her mid-seventies, she found out that there was truly a God, and He certainly did love her. Hopelessly addicted, there seemed to be no way to quit. God entered the picture and made a way where there seemed to be no way.